Tutu's Table

MEMORABLE MEALS AND FUN
CELEBRATIONS WITH FAMILY AND FRIENDS

JILL AKER-RAY
PHOTOGRAPHY BY STACEY SPRENZ

First Edition

ISBN: 978-1-957723-06-8 (hard cover)
        978-1-957723-07-5 (soft cover)

Aker-Ray, Jill.
Tutu's Table.

Edited by: Chris Kinsley
Photography by: Stacey Sprenz

Published by Warren Publishing
Charlotte, NC
www.warrenpublishing.net
Printed in the United States

To Mom,

For giving me life,
For nurturing and loving me unconditionally,
For teaching me life lessons,
For dedicating and sacrificing your entire life for the sake of your family,
For always embracing the best in people and the world,
And ... for making each day a memorable celebration!
I miss you every day.

Love forever,
Your Jilly

TABLE OF CONTENTS

THE "BOLOGNA FACE"

INSPIRED BY MOM—A.K.A. TUTU—THE MASTER
OF BOLOGNA FACES, WHO ALWAYS MADE
MEALS FUN AND PLAYFUL!

"ALWAYS, WHENEVER POSSIBLE ...
PLAY WITH YOUR FOOD"
–JILL AKER-RAY

TUTU DEFINED

HAWAIIAN SLANG MEANING
GRANDMOTHER OR GRANDFATHER

In the Hawaiian language, the word *tutu* for grandmother is of recent origin; it's something of a novelty, yet it is used frequently and with great fondness instead of *Grandma* by people on the islands.

In Hawaii, Tutu is often used for grandparents of both genders although, technically, grandmothers are called Tutu Wahine and grandfathers are called Tutu Kane.

When my daughter was born in 1992, my mom was so excited to become a grandmother! But because Taylor already had a *Grandma*, my mom decided to go with the name "Granna."

Fast-forward to 1995 when her grandson, Tyler, was born in Hawaii, where my brother-in-law and sister were stationed in the Army. The above definitions for "tutu" were endearing and a special reminder of Tyler's birthplace, so she became "Tutu" to him.

When Taylor was about four, she asked why Tyler called their grandmother Tutu and she had to call her Granna. I told her she didn't have to call her Granna, she could call her Tutu as well.

My mom was the very essence of the name; with a floral muumuu and bare feet, she was a happy and playful soul.

She was born Harriet Roseanne DeBard. Her beloved nieces and nephews called her Aunt Harriet, her friends and neighbors called her Terri, her co-workers called her Mother Aker. By the end of her life, everyone called her Tutu ... and there will never be another.

My mom was my hero.

Oh, don't misunderstand me. In the world's view, she didn't fit the description of "successful," as she had not hit the educational or career markers expected by society, and she made some choices that were less than steller. However, she showed me how to own up to and make the best of your life choices and make the decision to find joy in each day and the good in each person.

Mom was dealt some pretty tough blows throughout her life (physically, financially, and emotionally), but she *always* persevered and made the best of things. She bravely raised four children by herself and worked three or four jobs in order to make ends meet. She had the help of many loving people, including my big sister, friends, family, neighbors, fellow churchgoers, and co-workers. She never accepted help without giving twofold in return through her love, hospitality, generosity, and, without a doubt, food.

I remember my mom turning every occasion into a celebration of some sort. Sure, we had the typical birthdays, holidays, and Sunday dinners that most of us remember fondly. But then, there were the exceptional "celebrations." When she didn't have enough money to take us on a true vacation, she'd instead announce it was time for a "mystery trip." She loaded us all into her big old Ford LTD sedan and headed off to the beach or to nowhere in particular, creatively making it up as she went along.

On days when leftovers needed to be "sold" as delicious, she played restaurant with us, taking out her order pad and letting us know what "specials" were on the menu. We were never the wiser that she had no money for groceries. We just thought it was a fun game.

And on the nights that she proclaimed dinner was "bread and pull-it," anything you could pull out of the pantry or refrigerator and put on bread was your meal choice! Those are some of the best memories of my childhood. Why? Simply because of my mom's attitude toward them.

She ran a tight ship (because she had to), and the chores had to be done. She had barely a minute to spare, so she was organized and efficient. No matter how busy or tired she was, though, she always found time to celebrate her friends and family and make people feel special and loved. She always made birthday cakes for our teachers at school and for our dearest friends, aunts, uncles, nieces, nephews, and neighbors. Some remember those birthday cakes fondly, even to this day.

At the end of the school year, she would invite all the kids in each of our classes over to make "sundaes in the mouth." This tradition became very well-known at our elementary school, and our classmates looked forward to it all year. (Imagine a classroom room mom feeding a child a sundae with chocolate or caramel syrup, whipped cream, sprinkles, and a cherry, all while the child sat at the picnic table and leaned back, eating it as she made it!)

Mom ran a home day care when I was a toddler and had a birthday celebration for each child, as well as one for my great-grandmother, who loved to come over and watch us play. Mom would have our extended family over for supper most Sundays (though she was the one with the least time and money to do so) because she knew that "the memories we make" were the true riches in this world, and she seized every opportunity to make them.

From our traditional Fondue Party every summer to Swampwater and Skip-Bo with her friends and co-workers, Tutu always delighted in people's fun and laughter. She was a natural (and goofy) entertainer and prankster with a list of tricks too long to mention.

Despite her failing health toward the end of her life, she started a "Cane Club" for my grandmother's elderly bridge friends (my mom lived with and cared for my grandmother for many years). She would take them on a mystery trip once a month or serve a holiday meal around her kitchen table (like on Saint Patrick's Day when she colored the mashed potatoes and cake green and had silly things for them to do). Even when receiving chemotherapy, instead of being sad, she said, "Well, Jilly, you just never know who you might meet in here," and proceeded to comfort others having their first treatments, showing them where the snacks and drinks and blankets were.

Tutu truly chose *joy* every day and spread it to those around her. She is missed dearly, but her legacy teaches me daily lessons and will be treasured forever.

You'll find that this book is divided into sections according to seasonal celebrations instead of various food types. This is in honor of Tutu, who made every meal and occasion a cause for celebration. It is my heart's desire that you will be able to use some of these recipes and ideas to make special memories with those you love.

Because, as Tutu always said, "In the end, it's all about the memories you leave behind, so make them good ones."

May your tummy be full and your heart be content,

10   Tutu's Table

BABY BUNTING . . . Snug as a bug in a r
bright-eyed little Jill Aker rides the "grocery
ress" as she accompanies her mother, Mrs. J.
cer, 1821 Sanford St., on a shopping trip. The sh
g cart is a perfect snowmobile for Jill.

Jill Aker Ray 11

SIMPLE SUNDAY SUPPERS AND WEEKNIGHT FAVORITES

MOM'S MEATLOAF

PREP TIME: 5 Minutes
COOK TIME: 55–65 Minutes
SERVES: 8

There are so many variations of this classic American favorite, but this
is the basic recipe that often showed up on our dinner table to feed a
growing family of four kids. Serve it without mashed potatoes and gravy
(and a green vegetable).

INGREDIENTS

- 2 lbs. lean ground beef, ground turkey, meatloaf mix, or Beyond Burger (vegan substitute)
- 1 packet onion soup mix
- 2 eggs, beaten
- ⅓ cup ketchup (plus more for top)
- ¾ cup milk
- 2 Tbs. Worcestershire sauce
- 1½ cups bread crumbs, oats, or torn bread

INSTRUCTIONS

1. Preheat oven to 350 degrees.
2. Generously spray two loaf pans.
3. Mix all ingredients (except ground meat) gently until bread crumbs or oats are saturated with milk.
4. Gently add ground meat and blend well.
5. Fill loaf pans evenly and bake for 55–65 minutes.

SUNDAY POT ROAST

PREP TIME: 20 Minutes
COOK TIME: 4–8 Hours
SERVES: 8

The Crockpot slow cooker, branded in 1971 when I was just seven years old, was a relatively new appliance when I was growing up. For my mom, who was feeding four kids and juggling more than one job and many schedules, this was a lifesaving kitchen tool! One of the standard slow cooker meals was this pot roast, which provided a cozy, comforting meal in the snowy winters and an intoxicating aroma as we patiently waited for it to cook. We always enjoyed an extra meal from its tender roast or, even better, loose meat sandwiches.

INGREDIENTS

- 4–5 lb. bone-in chuck roast
- 2 Tbs. canola or vegetable oil
- 2 tsp. kosher salt
- 1 tsp. ground black pepper
- 1 tsp. dried thyme or Italian seasoning
- 1 lb. carrots, peeled and cut into 2"–3" chunks
- 2 stalks celery, cut into 2"–3" pieces
- 2 onions, peeled and cut into 2"–3" pieces
- 2 lbs. baby potatoes (red or Yukon Gold), cut in half if too large
- 2 cloves garlic, minced
- 2 cups beef broth
- 2 Tbs. Worcestershire Sauce
- 2 Tbs. cornstarch or Wondra flour
- 2 Tbs. cold water
- Fresh parsley, minced (optional)

INSTRUCTIONS

1. Dry chuck roast with paper towel, then season it with salt, pepper, and thyme or Italian seasoning.
2. Preheat a pan (or slow cooker insert if it's cooktop safe) to medium-high heat.
3. Add the oil. When it ripples, add the roast and brown for 4–5 minutes on each side.
4. Transfer to slow cooker and add carrots, celery, onion, garlic, and potatoes on top. Season with more salt and pepper.
5. Add beef broth and Worcestershire Sauce around the outside edges and cover. Set timer for 4 hours on high or 8 hours on low.
6. One hour prior to cooking completion, create a slurry by mixing cornstarch or flour with cold water. Add slurry to slow cooker to thicken sauce and re-cover for the last hour. Sprinkle with parsley and serve.

BAKED LEMON CHICKEN

PREP TIME: 5 Minutes
COOK TIME: 35–45 Minutes
SERVES: 4–6

I used to love the aroma of lemon, garlic, herbs, and roasting chicken wafting through the house. Whenever Tutu baked this, I knew company was coming for Sunday dinner!

INGREDIENTS

- 2½ lbs. skin-on, bone-in chicken breasts or thighs (I prefer thighs.)
- 2–4 Tbs. olive oil or butter (I like a combo of both.)
- 2–4 Tbs. lemon juice (juice of ½–1 lemon)
- 1 Tbs. lemon pepper seasoning
- 1½ tsp. Lawry's Seasoned Salt
- 1 tsp. Italian seasoning
- Lemon slices
- Fresh herbs such as parsley, rosemary, oregano, etc. (optional)

INSTRUCTIONS

1. Preheat oven to 400 degrees.
2. Pat the chicken dry with paper towels and place on a baking sheet or 9" x 13" pan. Spray with cooking spray.
3. Drizzle the olive oil over both sides of the chicken, rubbing to coat well. Then turn skin-side up. Drizzle with lemon juice.
4. In another small bowl, stir together the lemon pepper seasoning, seasoned salt, and Italian seasoning.
5. Sprinkle the spices evenly over the chicken. Cover with pats of butter (optional) and lemon slices.
6. Bake in preheated oven for 35–45 minutes until the chicken has reached an internal temperature of 165 degrees.
7. Garnish with a sprinkle of fresh herbs and serve with creamy mashed potatoes or rice to soak up the tart and herbaceous juices.

GRAVY

- ⅓ up flour
- ⅓ cup steak drippings
- 1–2 cups whole milk
- salt and pepper

1. After all meat is fried, pour off the drippings into a heat-resistant bowl or measuring cup and set aside.
2. Without cleaning the pan, return it to the stove over medium-low heat.
3. Add ¼ cup grease back to the pan and allow to heat up.
4. Sprinkle ⅓ cup flour evenly over the drippings. Using a whisk, mix flour with grease, creating a golden-brown paste. Keep cooking until it reaches a deep golden-brown color. If paste seems more oily than pasty, sprinkle in another tablespoon of flour and whisk.
5. Whisking constantly, pour in milk. Cook to thicken the gravy. Be prepared to add more milk if it becomes overly thick. Add salt and pepper and cook for 5–10 minutes until gravy is smooth and thick. Be sure to taste to make sure gravy is sufficiently seasoned.
6. Serve meat next to a big side of mashed potatoes. Pour gravy over both!

COUNTRY-FRIED STEAK

PREP TIME: 15 Minutes
COOK TIME: 10–14 Minutes
SERVES: 4–6

In our house, this was lovingly referred to as "pound steak" for its need to be pounded thin with a kitchen mallet to tenderize the otherwise tough round steak. These days, it's easy to skip this step by purchasing cube steaks that are already tenderized by a machine. Country-fried steak was *always* my requested birthday dinner, and I loved having Tutu's homemade mashed potatoes and green beans nuzzled in next to it.

INGREDIENTS
- 3 lbs. cube steak (extra-tenderized round steak)
- 3 ½ cups buttermilk
- 2 large eggs
- 3 cups all-purpose flour
- Lawry's Seasoned Salt
- ¼ tsp. cayenne pepper
- Lots of black pepper (*lots*)
- Canola or vegetable oil for frying

INSTRUCTIONS
1. Begin with an assembly line of four dishes for breading the meat: the meat in one; the buttermilk-egg mixture in one; the flour mixed with spices in one; and one clean plate at the end for the breaded meat.
2. Work one piece of meat at a time. Dry the meat thoroughly with paper towel.
3. Season both sides with salt and pepper, then dip in the buttermilk-egg mixture. Next, dip the meat in the plate of seasoned flour mixture, turning to coat thoroughly.
4. Shake off excess flour.
5. Place the meat back into the buttermilk-egg mixture, turning to coat.
6. Dredge back in the flour mixture and turn to coat.
7. Place breaded meat on sheet pan, then repeat steps with remaining meat.
8. Heat oil in a large cast-iron skillet over medium heat. Drop in a few sprinkles of flour to make sure it's sufficiently hot.
9. Cook meat, three pieces at a time, until edges start to look golden brown; around 2 ½–3 minutes each side.
10. Remove to a paper towel-lined plate and keep warm. Repeat until all meat is cooked.

MIDWEST MEAT SAUCE

PREP TIME: 20–30 Minutes
COOK TIME: 1 Hour
SERVES: 4–6

This spaghetti sauce in no way represents a true Italian recipe, but it was hearty, full of flavor, and beloved by many, including my siblings and me. Tutu jarred and tagged it as a gift of homemade comfort food for many a neighbor or loved one. I may roll my eyes now at the canned mushrooms, but it isn't her authentic recipe without them.

INGREDIENTS

- 1 Tbs. olive oil
- 1 lb. ground chuck
- 6 oz. can tomato paste
- 3 tomato paste cans of water
- 28 oz. can good quality whole tomatoes, hand crushed
- 1 small can mushrooms (Tutu used Pennsylvania Dutchman brand.) or 8 oz. fresh mushrooms, diced
- 1 green pepper, diced
- 1 small onion, diced
- 1–2 cloves garlic, minced
- ¼ tsp. red pepper flakes
- ½ tsp. salt
- ½ tsp. oregano
- ½ tsp. basil
- 1 Tbs. sugar
- ⅛ tsp. freshly grated nutmeg (optional)
- Plenty of Parmesan cheese, freshly grated (though Tutu could only afford the store-bought jar of Parmesan)

INSTRUCTIONS

1. Prep all ingredients. Mince garlic; dice onion, pepper, and mushrooms; open jars; and crush tomatoes.
2. Brown ground chuck and lightly drain fat if necessary. (Don't forget the flavor is in there!)
3. Set meat aside in a colander. In the same pan, sauté onion, green pepper, and mushrooms over medium heat until slightly soft. Add garlic and sauté another minute or two, being careful not to burn.
4. Add meat back in with vegetables, then add crushed tomatoes, tomato paste, all spices, sugar, and nutmeg (optional). Bring heat up to a slight boil, incorporate all ingredients, and turn on low. Cover slightly and simmer for an hour or so. Taste and adjust seasonings as needed.
5. Serve over pasta or spaghetti squash and sprinkle Parmesan on top. Add a crisp garden salad plus garlic bread for a crowd-pleasing family dinner.

AMERICAN GOULASH

PREP TIME: 15 Minutes
COOK TIME: 45 Minutes
SERVES: 6–8

The simplest version of this Americanized recipe was a staple in our household. My dad loved it and insisted on using stewed tomatoes in it. It was comforting and hearty, as well as an economical way to feed a big family. This recipe brings back lots of fond memories for me. (Indulge me for adding the smoked paprika to pay homage to the authentic Hungarian version.)

INGREDIENTS

- 1 Tbs. olive oil
- 1–1 ½ lbs. lean ground beef or meat substitute
- 1 yellow or Vidalia onion, diced
- 3–4 cloves garlic, minced
- 1 large or 2 small bell peppers, diced (I like to use one red and one green.)
- 1–2 tsp. paprika (I love the smoked version.)
- 1 tsp. Lawry's Seasoned Salt to taste
- 1 tsp. Italian seasoning
- 2 bay leaves
- ½ cup water
- 1 beef bouillon cube
- 2 (14.5 oz.) cans stewed tomatoes
- 15 oz. can tomato sauce
- 1 Tbs. Worcestershire sauce
- ½ lb. macaroni, cooked for 2 minutes less than package directions

INSTRUCTIONS

1. Dice the onions and peppers and mince the garlic.
2. Heat the pan to medium. Add the oil. Sauté onions and peppers in a large nonstick pot until translucent (about 2 minutes).
3. Add paprika and Italian seasoning and let the spices bloom for about 30 seconds.
4. Turn heat to medium-high, add ground beef, and cook thoroughly.
5. Add the rest of the ingredients *except* macaroni.
6. Heat to boil, then turn to a low simmer and cover. Cook for about 30 minutes, stirring occasionally. Remove bay leaves.
7. Meanwhile, cook, drain, and rinse macaroni. Add to goulash just before serving.

** This is really good served with a little grated cheese on top.

RED CARPET AWARDS NIGHT

TRUFFLED POPCORN

PREP TIME: 5 Minutes
MAKES: 1 (If I'm eating it)

Popcorn is my absolute favorite snack of all time (and also my Great Dane, Luna's, fave!). This is no surprise, as popcorn was a special treat on Sunday nights at my grandparents' house. We'd get so excited when we got special permission to enjoy this freshly popped and generously buttered treat, along with our choice of Faygo orange or grape pop, while sitting in front of the console TV watching *The Wonderful World of Disney* or *The Ed Sullivan Show*. Those memories come back every time I make a batch in my whirly popcorn popper.

INGREDIENTS

- ½ cup popcorn kernels
- 3 Tbs. oil (vegetable, coconut, olive, avocado, or safflower) or ghee
- ½–1 tsp. salt
- 2-3 Tbs. butter, melted (optional, but encouraged)

Optional:
Truffle salt
Edible gold dust

INSTRUCTIONS

1. Heat a Whirley Pop or large solid nonstick pan with a lid to medium heat and add oil.
2. Place 1 kernel of popcorn in pan until it pops, then add remaining popcorn plus half of the regular salt. Whirl on medium heat or shake frequently in regular pan until almost all popping stops or until it pops only every 4–5 seconds.
3. Remove from heat and transfer to a large bowl. Add butter and stir gently with a butter knife or spatula until butter coats kernels evenly.
4. Taste and adjust for salt. Then sprinkle with truffle salt and gold dust for a festive and glamorous Oscar-worthy snack!

ROASTED SHRIMP WITH YUM YUM SAUCE

PREP TIME: 5 Minutes
COOK TIME: 8–10 Minutes
SERVINGS: 3–4 as Appetizer

We did not live a life of luxury, but my mom always tried to indulge us in "the good life" whenever possible. She loved shrimp cocktail and would always include it on our Christmas Eve buffet before Midnight Mass. When I became a personal chef, I decided it just wasn't enough for me to serve it that way, so I came up with this variation instead. The shrimp becomes the excuse for the sauce, and vice versa. I recommend using the sauce for everything!

INGREDIENTS

- 1 lb. large shrimp, peeled and deveined, tail on
- 2 Tbs. olive oil
- 2 cloves garlic, minced
- 1 tsp. favorite spice blend (I like a smoky butt rub seasoning or a GOYA blend in orange packet.)
- Sea salt and freshly ground black pepper to taste (if using a salted spice blend, omit the sea salt)
- 2 Tbs. lemon juice or juice of one lemon
- 2 Tbs. parsley leaves, chopped, for garnish

INSTRUCTIONS

1. Preheat oven to 400 degrees.
2. Place shrimp in a single layer on foil-lined baking sheet. Add olive oil, then toss to coat. Sprinkle with garlic, spice blend, salt, and pepper.
3. Place into oven and roast just until pink, firm, and cooked through, about 8–10 minutes.
4. Stir in lemon juice.
5. Serve immediately, garnished with parsley if desired.
6. Optional: Chill for 1 hour or overnight in a sealed container to serve like traditional shrimp cocktail.
7. Use Yum-Yum sauce (recipe below) for dipping.

YUM YUM SAUCE

- 1 cup quality mayonnaise
- 1 Tbs. ketchup
- 1 Tbs. butter, melted
- 1 Tbs. mirin (wine)
- 2 tsp. rice vinegar
- ¼ tsp. smoked paprika
- ¾ tsp. garlic powder
- ¾ tsp. onion powder
- 1 Tbs. granulated sugar
- 1–2 Tbs. water, or until desired consistency is reached

Optional: Add a few splashes of hot sauce or dash of cayenne pepper for heat.

1. Mix together all ingredients except water until thoroughly blended and smooth. Add hot sauce (optional).
2. Add water as needed for desired consistency.
3. Chill for at least 2 hours in refrigerator. Keep stored in sealed container in refrigerator for up to 7 days.

CHAMPAGNE PUNCH

PREP TIME: 10–12 Minutes
SERVES: About 20

This is one of my original recipes, but versions of it have been popular in my family for decades. Nothing screams "celebration" louder than champagne and a punch bowl! Mixing this up as a signature drink eliminates the need for tending bar and allows you more time with guests.

INGREDIENTS

- ½ cup water
- ½ cup sugar
- 2 bottles (750 mL.) brut Champagne, chilled
- 1 ½ cups white rum or vodka
- 1 ¼ cups pomegranate juice
- 1 large lime, thinly sliced
- Pomegranate seeds
- Fresh mint leaves
- 1 ice block or ice ring

INSTRUCTIONS

1. Bring ½ cup water and sugar to boil in small saucepan, stirring until sugar dissolves. Simmer 5 minutes. Cool syrup completely.
2. Combine Champagne, rum or vodka, and pomegranate juice in punch bowl. Add enough syrup to sweeten to taste.
3. Mix in lime slices, pomegranate seeds, and mint leaves. Add ice block to bowl.

GRANDMA DEBARD'S CHOCOLATE SAUCE

PREP TIME: 5 minutes
COOK TIME: 5 minutes
MAKES: About 1 cup

INGREDIENTS

- 10 Tbs. granulated sugar
- 2–3 Tbs. cocoa powder
- 2 Tbs. flour
- 2 Tbs. butter
- 1 tsp. vanilla extract
- ½–1 cup milk

INSTRUCTIONS

1. Mix all ingredients in a saucepan. Boil over *low* heat, stirring constantly until smooth and thickened. Serve over vanilla pudding, crepes, ice cream, banana slices, or (in the South) biscuits.

VANILLA CUSTARD WITH CHOCOLATE SAUCE

PREP TIME: 10 Minutes
COOK TIME: 5 Minutes
MAKES: 4

My grandma used to make her homemade vanilla pudding and this special chocolate sauce to top it with. My little sister, Ann, would always request this as her birthday "cake." You might wonder, *Why not a real cake?* Make it, taste it, and you will understand why! My cousin Carrie now makes this sauce, keeping the tradition alive but wisely substituting boxed vanilla pudding as a modern and timesaving substitute for the custard!

INGREDIENTS

- 2 cups whole milk
- 2 tsp. vanilla extract
- ⅔ cup sugar
- ¼ tsp. salt
- ¼ cup cornstarch
- 4 large egg yolks at room temperature
- 1 Tbs. unsalted butter, diced

Optional: bourbon

INSTRUCTIONS

1. Heat milk and vanilla extract to a low simmer in a heavy-bottomed medium saucepan. Do not let boil; heat until little bubbles form around the edges of the pan.
2. Meanwhile, place sugar, cornstarch, and salt into the bowl of a stand mixer fitted with the whisk attachment or into a large mixing bowl. Whisk dry ingredients until mixed. Add egg yolks and blend until a pale yellow.
3. Slowly pour milk mixture into eggs while whisking at a low speed. Do not mix too fast, or it will froth and foam. Blend until mixed.
4. Transfer mixture back to the saucepan and cook over medium-low heat for 3–5 minutes or until thickened. Whisk continually to prevent mixture from scalding.
5. As soon as mixture thickens, remove from heat and whisk in butter (or bourbon if desired). My grandmother did not add either butter or bourbon, but I favor bourbon.
6. Serve immediately, topped with Grandma DeBard's Chocolate Sauce or transfer to a clean bowl and cover with plastic wrap. Press plastic wrap into the custard mixture so there is no air between the two. This prevents the filmy skin that can develop. To set faster, place in small ramekins or bowls.

TIP
Start by scalding the milk and vanilla. You'll need to have hot milk to make this work. I use vanilla extract for this recipe, but you can also use a vanilla bean.

BASICS OF CHEESE AND CHARCUTERIE

Charcuterie and cheese boards are my go-to choice for easy, elegant, no-stress entertaining. You can load them up with all your favorite cheeses, cured meats, seasonal fruit, nuts, and spreads. Add some good friends, wine, and baguettes, and you have a fabulous party!

INGREDIENTS

- **Cheeses—at least 3 types**
  Soft, creamy, mild, sharp, funky, smoked
- **Charcuterie (cured meats)— at least 3 types**
  Salty, spicy, rich (fatty)
- **Savory**
  Cheeses and Meats
- **Sweet**
  Berries, grapes, jams and preserves, dried fruit (Don't forget chocolate and cookies or sweets.)
- **Sour (pickled items)**
  Cornichons, olives, pickled veggies
- **Verying textures (crunchy or soft)**
  Nuts, breadsticks, soft bread, crackers

- **Varying heights**
  Like a tablescape: tall, short, and medium
- **Color palette**
  Including colorful fruits, vegetables, meats, cheeses, etc.
- **Separation of dry and wet items**
  Put olives, pickles, and other briny items in individual containers to prevent them from leaking onto crackers and bread.
- **Special items for various tastes and diets**
  Add gluten-free crackers, a vegan dip like hummus, and some individually wrapped items. Ask about nut allergies to help all your guests have safe options.

BASIC FUDGE RECIPE

PREP TIME: 15 Minutes
CHILL TIME: 1 Hour
MAKES: 24–36 pieces

Aunt Colleen was the cool aunt! We all adored her because she not only had fashion sense and the latest and greatest gifts, but she also hosted the best parties and cooked every part of the menu! She was a beautiful person inside and out, plus made the most delicious fudge ever! I'm thankful to my cousin Erika for passing on this recipe so we can keep her memory alive. It is a treasure to have her recipe and be able to pass on her love of feeding family and friends.

INGREDIENTS

- 3 cups granulated sugar
- ¾ cup (1 ½ sticks) butter
- ⅔ cup evaporated milk
- Small, 7 oz. jar marshmallow creme
- 1 tsp. pure vanilla extract
- 2 cups chocolate chips, peanut butter chips or white chocolate chips
- 1 cup chopped nuts (optional)

INSTRUCTIONS

1. Grease a 9" x 13" pan. For added ease, line the pan with waxed paper and spray again lightly. (This makes it easy to lift fudge out of the pan and cut into squares.)
2. In a medium saucepan, add sugar, butter, and evaporated milk. Stir together and bring to a boil, stirring for about 5 minutes.
3. Remove from heat and add chips, marshmallow creme, vanilla, and nuts. Stir to melt and incorporate all ingredients.
4. Immediately pour into the prepared pan and smooth evenly with a rubber or silicone spatula.
5. Refrigerate for at least 1 hour. Cover it once fudge is cooled and set.
6. Lift out of pan and cut into squares to serve.

THE ANNUAL CHILI COOK-OFF

BASIC CHILI

PREP TIME: 35 Minutes
COOK TIME: 20–30 Minutes (Or More)
SERVES: 4–6

This is what I grew up knowing as chili; it was simmering on the stove many a school night. It's as basic and mild as chili gets, but it's the only one my daughter Taylor will eat to this day! This recipe works as both a satisfying meal and an easy-to-use topping for a kid-friendly taco salad!

INGREDIENTS

- 1 lb. ground beef (I like 85% lean meat/ 15% fat because I don't have to drain it.)
- 1 sweet onion, diced
- 1 green pepper, diced
- 1 jalapeño, diced small (optional)
- 2 cloves fresh garlic, minced, or 1 tsp. granulated garlic
- 2 cans stewed tomatoes (hand crushed, if you like it less chunky)
- 2 Tbs. tomato paste (I use the tube of tomato paste.)
- 2 cans kidney beans, pinto, or black beans, undrained
- 2 Tbs. sugar (optional)
- 1 packet chili seasoning mix
- Salt and pepper to taste

** You can add cocoa powder and cumin and extra chili powder if desired.

INSTRUCTIONS

1. Heat a heavy Dutch oven or pot over medium heat. Add ground beef, onion, green pepper, and jalapeño. Brown the beef and sauté the vegetables for about 19 minutes.
2. Add garlic cloves or granulated garlic and chili packet, cooking for 2–3 minutes to bloom the spices.
3. Add stewed tomatoes and mash using a potato masher.
4. Add beans, tomato paste, and sugar, cooking on medium-low heat for 20–30 minutes and stirring occasionally. Taste and adjust for additional spices and salt and pepper.
5. Serve with cornbread, saltines, or tortilla chips as well as cheddar cheese and sour cream.

** Chili always tastes better the next day!

SKILLET CORNBREAD

PREP TIME: 5–10 Minutes
BAKE TIME: 25–30 Minutes
SERVES: 6–8

I must admit, we usually only had saltine crackers with chili during my childhood. But living in Charlotte for the past thirty years and embracing the Southern life, I've learned that chili cook-offs would not be the same without cornbread for dipping or crumbling into a big bowl of chili! This is one of my favorite easy versions, and I'm proud to use Jiffy mix, as the company is located in Michigan!

INGREDIENTS

- 2 boxes Jiffy cornbread mix
- ½ cup milk or buttermilk
- ½ cup sour cream
- 3 Tbs. honey
- 2 eggs
- ¼ cup butter (to melt in skillet)
- Diced jalapeños, green chiles, and cheddar (optional)

INSTRUCTIONS

1. Preheat the oven to 375 degrees. Prepare a skillet by preheating it in the oven, adding butter to it, and putting it back in the oven to melt the butter.
2. Meanwhile, mix together the cornbread mix, milk, sour cream, honey, and eggs. (Add jalapeños, green chiles, and cheddar if using.) Pour into prepared skillet.
3. Bake for 25–30 minutes until fairly firm to the touch and golden brown.
4. Remove from oven and let cool 5 minutes. Run knife around edge of skillet and carefully invert cornbread onto a cutting board. Slice to serve.

HOT DOG CHILI SAUCE

PREP TIME: 10–20 Minutes
COOK TIME: 20 Minutes
SERVES: 6–12

A good quality all-beef hot dog was something my mom *loved*! I have fond memories of going with my siblings to G&L restaurant from the time I could barely peek over the counter. It was famous for its Greek chili dog, or Coney dog, that is popular in the Detroit area. This is my simple version of a recipe that has a similar taste profile. I hope if my mom could taste it, she would approve.

INGREDIENTS

- 1 lb. lean ground beef (85% lean meat/15% fat or 90% lean meat/10% fat)
- ¼ tsp. salt
- ¾ tsp. baking soda
- Water (enough to cover the meat)
- 1 medium Vidalia onion or sweet onion, finely diced or grated
- 2 cloves of garlic, finely diced
- 1 Tbs. olive oil
- 1½ cups ketchup
- 2 Tbs. tomato paste
- 1 Tbs. prepared yellow mustard (or favorite mustard)
- ½ tsp. salt
- ½ tsp. pepper
- 2 tsp. chili powder
- ¼ tsp. cinnamon
- 1 Tbs. Worcestershire sauce
- 1–2 Tbs. sugar (optional)

INSTRUCTIONS

1. Place lean ground beef in a bowl, mix in baking soda and salt, and cover with water. Use a wooden spoon or your hands to break up the beef. Set aside for about 20 minutes.**
2. Over medium heat, sauté diced onion and garlic in olive oil in a large sauté pan or Dutch oven.
3. Once the onion and garlic are soft, add the ground beef and water to the pan. Cook about 5 minutes, until the beef is no longer pink on the outside.
4. Add ketchup, tomato paste, mustard, salt, pepper, chili powder, cinnamon, and Worcestershire sauce. (Add sugar if using.)
5. Reduce heat and simmer for 20 minutes, stirring frequently until mixture has thickened and reduced and the beef is cooked through.

TIP
** This will make a thick, tender, and smooth chili sauce.

MOLASSES COOKIES

PREP TIME: 15–20 Minutes
COOK TIME: 8–10 Minutes
MAKES: 2½ dozen Cookies

These cookies were my brother Danny's favorite. He always asked my mom to make them, but we had no written recipe for them after her passing. I was able to tease and tweak this recipe and make them for him after he was diagnosed with cancer and wanted some special treats (and he gave me rave reviews, which was a huge compliment). They will always remind me of my love for him.

INGREDIENTS

- 2 cups all-purpose flour
- 2 tsp. baking soda
- ½ tsp. ground cinnamon
- 1 tsp. ground ginger
- ½ tsp. kosher salt
- 1 large egg
- ½ cup (1 stick) unsalted butter, melted
- ⅓ cup granulated sugar
- ⅓ cup light or dark molasses
- ¼ cup dark brown sugar, packed
- Coarse sugar or raw sugar
  (for rolling)

INSTRUCTIONS

1. Place oven racks in lower and upper thirds of oven; preheat to 375 degrees. In a small bowl, whisk flour, baking soda, cinnamon, ginger, and salt. In a medium bowl, whisk egg, butter, granulated sugar, brown sugar, and molasses. Mix dry mixture into wet mixture until just combined.

2. Place sugar in a shallow bowl. Scoop out dough by the tablespoonful and roll into balls (if dough is sticky, chill 20 minutes). Roll dough balls in sugar and place on 2 parchment-lined baking sheets, spacing 2 inches apart.

3. Bake cookies, halfway through baking time rotate baking sheets, until cookies are puffed, cracked, and just barely set around the edges, about 8–10 minutes. (Overbaked cookies won't be chewy.)

4. Transfer to a rack to cool.

5. Store in a cookie tin to keep consistency soft and chewy.

BAKED POTATO SOUP

PREP TIME: 20 Minutes
COOK TIME: 30–40 Minutes
SERVES: 6–8

This is one of the first recipes I made as a newlywed, after learning that Dave (my husband) loved potato soup. It became a favorite of the entire family, as well as our neighbors. Its simplicity and comforting effects make it a crowd favorite!

INGREDIENTS

- 1 sweet onion, minced
- ¼ cup carrots, minced
- ¼ cup celery, minced
- 4 Tbs. butter
- 4 Tbs. flour
- Spices such as salt, pepper, chili powder, cayenne, granulated garlic and paprika to taste
- 10 oz. vegetable or chicken broth
- 3 cups whole or 2% milk
- 4–6 large baking potatoes, peeled and cubed
- 1 cup sharp cheddar, Colby-Jack, or Mexican blend cheese, grated
- Chives, chopped
- Bacon, crumbled

INSTRUCTIONS

1. In large saucepan over medium heat, sauté onions, carrots, and celery in butter stirring occasionally until softened. Add flour and seasonings, stirring frequently for 1 minute to form a blonde roux.
2. Add broth, milk, and potatoes; heat to a boil. Reduce heat to low; cover and simmer for about 20 minutes or until potatoes are tender, stirring often.
3. Remove from heat, ladle into bowls, and top with cheese, bacon, and chives.

TUTU'S VEGETABLE SOUP

PREP TIME: 15 Minutes
COOK TIME: 2.5 hours
SERVES: 8–10

This was a staple on our stove in the wintertime during my childhood. I crave it to this day when I need something warm and loving in my tummy. I wanted to make changes to this recipe to enhance or update it, but since my copy is written in my mom's hand, I cannot bring myself to alter it.

INGREDIENTS

- 3 lb. boneless chuck roast
- 1 onion, chopped
- 1 tsp. garlic salt
- ½ tsp. pepper
- 2 tsp. Lawry's Seasoned Salt
- 46 oz. can tomato juice
- 3 qts. water
- 2 packages frozen vegetables (large bags)
- Plus any other vegetables you like that aren't in frozen package.
- (Tutu always added more potatoes and a small can of lima beans or okra.)

INSTRUCTIONS

1. Cook meat in simmering water with onion, salts, pepper, and tomato juice until tender and falling off the bone, about 2–2½ hours.
2. Take meat out of pot, cool and tear apart, and return to broth.
3. Bring to a boil and add the vegetables. Boil about 10 minutes.

BEER CHEESE SOUP

PREP TIME: 20 Minutes
COOK TIME: 20–25 Minutes
SERVES: 4–6

This recipe is from my all-time favorite hometown restaurant in Muskegon, Michigan. It's the first place I head to when visiting (after seeing my family, of course!) and always involves at least one cup of this delicious cheesy soup. My mom loved it also, and we have wonderful fond memories of special meals together at Hearthstone. I am forever grateful to have this treasured recipe.

INGREDIENTS

- ¼ stick of butter
- 1 medium onion
- 1 celery stalk
- 1 good-size carrot or a couple of small ones
- 2 gloves garlic, minced
- ¼ cup flour
- 3 tsp. dry mustard
- ¼ tsp. white pepper
- 2 dashes of Worcestershire
- 2 cups half-and-half
- 1 cup reduced-sodium chicken broth
- 24 oz. sharp cheddar, shredded, or melting cheese, cubed
- 12 oz. of your favorite beer
- Cheese popcorn for garnish

INSTRUCTIONS

1. Melt butter in a Dutch oven. Put onion, celery, and carrots in a food processor. Pulse until finely chopped. Add to melted butter and sauté until tender, about 5 minutes.

2. Add flour, pepper, mustard, and Worcestershire. Stir constantly for 1 minute.

3. Gradually add in half-and-half and chicken broth. Stir until combined. Cook 15 minutes until soup is thickened.

4. Add cheese and once it is melted use an immersion blender to purée all the vegetables until smooth. Add 1 room-temperature beer. Cook 8 minutes, stirring frequently. Do not boil.

5. Garnish with cheese popcorn.

EASTER CELEBRATION

HERB-ENCRUSTED GRILLED LEG OF LAMB

PREP TIME: 10 Minutes (Plus 12 Hours Marinating Time)
COOK TIME: 35–40 Minutes (+10 Minutes Resting Time)
SERVES: 10–12

It's an Easter family tradition that started early in our marriage with a great recipe. It's a mouthwatering way to enjoy the grilled lamb accented with a mango chutney for dipping. Both my mom and mother-in-law would wait at the dinner table like little kids on Christmas morning! Roasted potatoes and artichokes or asparagus are wonderful spring accompaniments to this bold, rich meat.

INGREDIENTS

- 5–6 lb. leg of lamb, trimmed of excess fat, boned, and butterflied
- Vegetable oil for brushing the grill rack
- Herbed Olive Oil Marinade Paste (see recipe below) **
- Fruit chutney (We use Major Grey's mango chutney).

INSTRUCTIONS

1. Prepare the marinade paste as directed.
2. Quickly rinse the lamb under cold running water and pat dry with paper towels. Place in a shallow, nonreactive container and rub all over with the marinade paste. Cover and refrigerate overnight or at least 12 hours. Return to room temperature before cooking.
3. Prepare a grill for moderate indirect grilling and place an drip pan under the area where the meat will be in order to catch oil dripping and reduce flare-ups.
4. Once the fire is ready, lightly brush the grill rack with vegetable oil. Place lamb on the grill rack, cover the grill, and cook, turning several times until done to preference, about 35–40 minutes total for medium

rare. Remove lamb from grill, place on cutting board, and tent with foil. Let stand for about 10 minutes. Thinly slice and plate, drizzle with some of the drippings, and serve with chutney alongside.

HERBED OLIVE OIL MARINADE PASTE
Makes 1 ¼ cup

This is the perfect way to season your boneless leg of lamb to achieve mouthwatering flavor.

- ¼ cup fruity olive oil, preferably extra-virgin
- 2 Tbs. lemon juice
- ¼ cup herbs de Provence
- 4 tsp. garlic, minced
- Salt and freshly ground pepper (plenty of it!)
- ¼ tsp. cayenne pepper (optional)

In a nonreactive bowl, combine all ingredients including salt and pepper to taste. Blend well. Makes about 1 ¼ cups.

"RITZY" BAKED FISH

PREP TIME: 5 Minutes
COOK TIME: 15 Minutes
SERVES: 4–8

Tutu made lots of fried perch and smelt from the Great Lakes, but this may have been my first experience of tasting fish from the ocean. Remember orange roughy, the very mild white fish that was popular back in the 1970s? My mom made this super-easy dish pretty often for us and especially when my great-aunt visited from Pasadena! Fancy it up with a local vegetable in season and some rice pilaf or couscous blend. Feel free to substitute any mild fish—sole, perch, flounder and tilapia are good choices.

INGREDIENTS

- 8 thin mild white fish filets (orange roughy, sole, perch, flounder, tilapia or swai), about 2 lbs.
- 2 sleeves Ritz Crackers or similar crackers, crushed
- 4 eggs, whipped and seasoned with salt and pepper
- 4 Tbs. butter, melted
- Lemon wedges

INSTRUCTIONS

1. Preheat oven to 350 degrees.
2. Set up a wire rack over a sheet pan. Spray with cooking spray.
3. Rinse fish filets and pat dry with paper towels.
4. Place eggs in one pan and crush crackers in another. Dip filet in eggs, then put into pan of cracker crumbs and pat to make crumbs stick.
5. Place filet on rack and repeat with all eight filets.
6. Drizzle with melted butter.
7. Bake for 12–15 minutes; serve with lemon wedges.

SIMPLY ROASTED VEGETABLES

PREP TIME: 15 Minutes
COOK TIME: About 35 Minutes
SERVES: 6–8

Seasonal produce was plentiful when I was a child, with asparagus, carrots, and green beans taking center stage in the late spring. Roasting any vegetable makes it sweeter and more flavorful, so feel free to use this recipe for any of your favorites.

INGREDIENTS

- 3 Tbs. olive oil
- 2 Tbs. whole-grain Dijon mustard
- 3 tsp. apple cider vinegar or balsamic vinegar
- ½ tsp. dried thyme
- ¾ tsp. kosher salt
- ½ tsp. black pepper
- ½ tsp. dried rosemary
- ¼ tsp. dried basil
- 1 lb. cauliflower florets
- 1 lb. carrots
- 1 lb. asparagus, trimmed
- 8 oz. baby red potatoes, halved or quartered (optional)
- Minced fresh parsley for garnish

INSTRUCTIONS

1. Preheat oven to 450 degrees. Line a large baking sheet with parchment paper sprayed lightly with cooking spray. Set aside.
2. In a large mixing bowl, combine olive oil, mustard, vinegar, thyme, salt, pepper, rosemary, and basil, and whisk. Add asparagus, cauliflower, carrots, and potatoes, stirring to coat.
3. Spread vegetable mixture in a single layer on prepared baking sheet. Bake for 20 minutes, stir gently, then bake another 15 minutes.
4. Serve garnished with minced parsley if desired.

DEVILED EGGS

PREP TIME: 20–25 Minutes (Including boiling the eggs)
MAKES: 1 Dozen

I don't remember a family picnic or gathering without deviled eggs on the table. They were basic ones, so feel free to dress them up with the optional toppings below or one of your choosing! Make a double batch because they are always gone by the end of the party!

INGREDIENTS

- 6 large or extra-large eggs
- 3 Tbs. mayonnaise
- 1 tsp. yellow or Dijon mustard
- 1 tsp. apple cider vinegar
- Salt and pepper or seasoned salt to taste
- Paprika and dried or fresh chives for garnish

INSTRUCTIONS

1. Place eggs in a small or medium saucepan and cover with cold water. Heat water and eggs to boiling, then turn off heat and cover pan with lid. Set timer for 11 minutes.

2. Remove from heat and rinse eggs with very cold water or place in an ice bath for a few minutes. Once you can handle the warm eggs, peel them immediately. Either refrigerate peeled eggs until ready to assemble or assemble immediately.

3. Slice eggs in half horizontally and carefully remove the yolks into a small bowl. Mash egg yolks and add the mayo, mustard, vinegar, and seasonings to taste. Spoon yolk filling into eggs or use a piping bag or plastic bag to fill eggs.

4. Garnish with paprika and chives and enjoy!

TIP

Feel free to skip the garnish and do a fun toppings bar for your deviled eggs, including: crumbled bacon, herbs, shrimp, smoked salmon, shallots, sriracha, olives, shredded cheese, pickle relish, etc.

RHUBARB-STRAWBERRY CRISP

PREP TIME: 15 Minutes
COOK TIME: 40 Minutes
SERVINGS: 6–8

Growing up in Michigan, I always looked forward to rhubarb season and my Aunt Nancy's strawberry-rhubarb pie. She always made the perfect crust and mastered just the right balance of sweet strawberries and tart rhubarb in the filling! This recipe is a simpler version since I haven't mastered a piecrust. It's easy, and other seasonal fruit can be substituted.

INGREDIENTS

- 4 cups rhubarb, sliced
- 2 cups strawberries, sliced
- 1 cup sugar (I use about ¾ cup because I like it tart!)
- ⅓ cup flour for fruit
- 1 cup flour for streusel topping
- ½ tsp. cinnamon
- 1 cup brown sugar
- 1 cup old fashioned oats
- ¼ tsp. nutmeg (or repeat cinnamon)
- ½ cup (1 stick), butter, melted and cooled a bit

INSTRUCTIONS

1. Preheat oven to 350 degrees.
2. Spray a 9" x 13" pan with cooking spray or rub with canola oil.
3. In a large bowl, combine rhubarb, strawberries, sugar, ⅓ cup flour, and cinnamon. Transfer to prepared baking dish.
4. In another bowl combine remaining 1 cup flour with brown sugar, oats, and nutmeg. Add melted butter and blend to create a streusel. Sprinkle streusel over rhubarb mixture and bake at 350 degrees for 35–40 minutes or until fruit is bubbly and top is golden brown.

WALDORF SALAD

PREP TIME: 15 Minutes
SERVES: 8–10

This "fancy" salad was created for the Waldorf Astoria's debut event, a charity ball in honor of St. Mary's Hospital for Children on March 14, 1893. It certainly must've had a resurgence in the 1970s, as I don't remember an Easter celebration without it on the table! Feel free to make the topping separately and serve alongside to give guests healthy choices for this popular fruit salad. Tutu thought she was fancy when she served it on a lettuce leaf.

INGREDIENTS

- 2 tart apples, diced but not peeled
- 1 can mandarin oranges, drained
- 1 cup fresh or canned pineapple
- ½ cup mini marshmallows (optional)
- 2 tsp. lemon juice
- 1 cup celery, diced
- 1 cup grapes, halved
- ½ cup walnuts or pecans, toasted and roughly chopped
- ½ cup whipping cream (or 2 Tbs. Greek yogurt or sour cream)
- ¼ cup mayonnaise
- ½ tsp. kosher salt

INSTRUCTIONS

1. Add the diced apples to a large mixing bowl and sprinkle with the lemon juice. Toss to coat. Add the celery, other fruit, and nuts.
2. In another bowl, whip the whipping cream until peaks form, add the sugar, then gently fold in the mayonnaise (see TIP below).
3. Fold into the apple mixture.
4. Taste and adjust the seasoning to your liking.
5. Chill for 1 hour or overnight. Sprinkle with kosher salt just before serving to enhance flavors.

TIP

Instead of whipping cream, substitute 2 tablespoons plain Green yogurt or sour cream and fold together with the mayonnaise and sugar.

FUN AND GAMES

SWAMPWATER

PREP TIME: 5 Minutes
SERVES: 8–10

My mom didn't really drink alcohol, but she threw the best parties for her friends who did imbibe! I remember countless game nights with her girlfriends throughout the '70s and '80s that centered around a Swampwater theme! It was quite the trendy thing back then, and its main ingredient is Green Chartreuse, which is a liqueur that has been made by the Carthusian Monks since 1737.

INGREDIENTS

- 1 bottle Green Chartreuse
- 1 can (46–48 oz.) pineapple juice
- 1 12 oz. can limeade
- 4 limes, sliced
- Ice

INSTRUCTIONS

1. Mix all ingredients except ice.
2. Place ice into punch just before serving and also fill glasses with ice if desired.

TUTU'S DIET COKE

SERVES: 1
PREP TIME: 5 Seconds

Tutu was hardly ever seen without one of these by her side. It was not the best habit, but it gave her great pleasure in a very challenging life, raising four children by herself and working a third-shift job with the lack of sleep that accompanies it. She would keep the SOLO cup in the freezer and ask her grandkids, Taylor or Tyler, to bring one to her "stat." How I wish I could bring one to her again.

INGREDIENTS

- 12 oz. can Diet Coke
- Red SOLO cup
- Ice

INSTRUCTIONS

1. Keep SOLO cup in freezer (the original YETI, ha-ha).
2. Add ice.
3. Pop top on can.
4. Pour ice-cold Diet Coke over ice and enjoy with your favorite salty snack (see Truffled Popcorn recipe on page 47 or Bold and Spicy Chex Mix recipe on page 115).

WARM FRENCH ONION DIP

PREP TIME: 5 Minutes
COOK TIME: 20 Minutes
SERVES: 4–6

Jay's potato chips with cool French onion dip was a staple snack in our house. This warm version of the dip served with homemade chips is dressed up enough for a cocktail party but retains all the familiar flavors of the original.

INGREDIENTS

- 1 envelope Onion Recipe Soup & Dip Mix
- 16 oz. sour cream
- 2 cups Swiss cheese or your favorite cheese, shredded
- ¼ cup Hellmann's® Mayonnaise

INSTRUCTIONS

1. Preheat oven to 375 degrees.
2. Combine onion soup mix, sour cream, 1¾ cups Swiss cheese, and mayonnaise in a 1-quart casserole.
3. Bake 20 minutes or until heated through. Sprinkle with remaining ¼ cup Swiss cheese.
4. Serve with your favorite dippers.

FRESH FRUIT SALSA

PREP TIME: 10–15 Minutes
SERVES: 8–10

This recipe is very versatile and perfectly refreshing on the warm autumn days in North Carolina where apples are abundant and so is the sunshine we enjoy even in November. Feel free to substitute other fruits in season, like peaches, pears or berries.

INGREDIENTS

- 2 cups (about 2 medium apples) crunchy sweet apples, cored and diced
- ½ cup red bell pepper, diced
- ⅓ cup (from about 2 limes) fresh lime juice
- ¼ cup red onion, finely diced
- ¼ cup fresh cilantro, chopped
- 1 Tbs. honey
- ¼ tsp. salt
- ¼ tsp. freshly ground black pepper
- Stacey's Cinnamon Sugar Pita Chips

INSTRUCTIONS

1. Combine all the fruit salsa ingredients, stirring well to coat the apples with the lime juice.
2. Refrigerate until ready to serve (this can be prepared ahead of time).

BOLD AND SPICY CHEX MIX

PREP TIME: 10 Minutes
SERVES: About 24
MAKES: 13-14 Cups

Nowadays, you can buy Chex snack mix in a multitude of flavors—from savory to sweet, from sugared to hot. When I was growing up, this was a special treat made with care (and lots of stirring while it was baking low and slow). It was the perfect snack for game night or with drinks, and my mom made it with love and packed it in tins for friends and family at Christmastime. My brother Danny continued this tradition enabling us to enjoy this special treat as adults. This recipe uses the microwave to save a little time, but it can still be made in the oven if you prefer. Feel free to add your favorite snacks or nuts. I love Cheetos and extra rye bagel chips in mine.

INGREDIENTS

- 9 cups Chex cereal (I like equal parts corn, rice and wheat—but feel free to use what you like.)
- 2 cups Gardetto's snack mix or rye bagel chips
- 1 cup crunchy Cheetos
- 1 cup peanuts or nuts of your choice
- ½ cup butter, melted and hot
- ⅓ cup Worcestershire sauce
- 1½ Tbs. seasoned salt
- 1 tsp. garlic powder
- ⅛–¼ tsp. cayenne or red Aleppo pepper (optional)

INSTRUCTIONS

1. Add all snack ingredients to a large microwave-safe bowl and gently stir to combine.
2. In a medium saucepan, melt butter and add the Worcestershire, seasoned salt, garlic powder, and pepper (if using) and mix thoroughly.
3. Drizzle half of the hot mixture over the snack mix. Stir very gently with a rubber spatula so you don't break the Chex. Repeat with the remaining butter mixture and stir again until just combined.
4. Microwave on high for 5–6 minutes uncovered, stirring every 2 minutes.
5. Spread the mix out on a parchment-lined cookie sheet or sheet pan until it has cooled to room temperature.
6. Store in airtight container for up to 3 weeks.

NO-BAKE COOKIES

PREP TIME: 10 Minutes
MAKES: 2–3 Dozen

I first tasted these no-bake goodies in the cafeteria lunch line at my elementary school. "Buying" lunch was a luxury for me and my siblings, so I always grabbed one of these for my tray when available. I learned to make them at home in third grade, and they've been a go-to cookie ever since.

INGREDIENTS

- 2 cups sugar
- ½ cup milk
- ½ cup (1 stick) butter
- ¼ cup cocoa powder
- 3 cups quick oats
- 1 cup peanut butter
- 1 tsp. vanilla

INSTRUCTIONS

1. Line two baking sheets with parchment paper and set aside.
2. In a medium saucepan, bring sugar, milk, butter, and cocoa powder to a boil, stirring occasionally. Once the mixture is boiling, let it boil for 1 full minute, then remove from heat.
3. Add the oatmeal, peanut butter, and vanilla and stir until well combined.
4. Using a medium cookie scoop, measure out tablespoons of dough onto the prepared baking sheets. Let rest at room temperature until cool or place in refrigerator for quicker cooling.

OH HENRY! BARS

PREP TIME: 15 Minutes
MAKES: 12 Bars in 9" x 13" pan or 9 Bars in 8" x 8" pan

This after-school treat was (one of) my brother's favorites. It was also one of the first desserts I ever made because I was only allowed to use the stove top, but not the oven, until I was about ten. It was always requested for Danny's birthday, and I can understand why, as who can resist the combination of chocolate and peanut butter and crunchy cereal?

INGREDIENTS
- 1 cup sugar
- 1 cup light corn syrup
- 2 cups peanut butter
- 6 cups cornflakes
- 12 oz. package chocolate chips

INSTRUCTIONS
1. Mix sugar and corn syrup together in a large pan on stove and bring to a boil.
2. Remove from heat and add peanut butter.
3. Pour cornflakes into a large bowl.
4. Pour hot mixture over top and mix well.
5. Press into a greased 8" x 8" or 9" x 13" pan.
6. Melt chocolate chips in microwave.
7. Spread over cornflake mixture.
8. Allow to cool and set in refrigerator, then cut into squares.

UNCLE JIM'S KETTLE CORN

PREP TIME: About 30 Minutes
MAKES: 7 Cups

This recipe is a treasure from my great-grandmother and has been passed down and become the always-anticipated sweet treat from my Uncle Jim. I remember getting excited to see those wrapped popcorn balls in the basket at our Christmas gatherings and looking forward to the sweet, salty, and crunchy combination of my favorite snack—*popcorn*!

INGREDIENTS

- 1 ¼ cups sugar
- ⅓ cup light Karo syrup
- ⅓ cup water
- 1 stick butter (no substitutions)
- 1 Tbs. vanilla extract
- 7 cups popped corn (about 5 bags of microwave popcorn, though I prefer freshly popped; see Truffled Popcorn recipe, page 29)

INSTRUCTIONS

1. Mix sugar, Karo syrup, water, and butter on stove over low heat. Once incorporated, don't stir unless necessary because stirring will cool the mixture and take longer for the glaze to form.
2. Test by dripping small amounts of the syrup in water until it forms brittle strings. (On high-humidity days, cook a few minutes longer to ensure the "crack" candy-cooking stage.)
3. Remove from heat and add vanilla extract. In very large bowl, add this mixture to the popcorn and stir gently with a rubber spatula to incorporate. Spray or butter your hands or gloves and form popcorn balls if desired (if you can wait that long to dig in!).
4. Store in a tin or tightly sealed container.

BREAKFAST AT GRANDMA AND GRANDPA'S

SKILLET PONHAUS

PREP TIME: 45 Minutes (plus cooling time)
COOK TIME: 2+ Hours
MAKES: 2–3 Loaf Pans

This simple and hearty Pennsylvania Dutch recipe was a Sunday breakfast staple at Grandma and Grandpa's. Many times, we had to go to Grandma's during the week and help stir the cornmeal in, taking turns as necessary until it got so thick you couldn't even stir it. It is important to get it into the bread pans quickly so that it doesn't set up in the pot. Ponhaus is similar to the Southern breakfast staple, livermush, or Pennsylvania's scrapple, but it doesn't contain pork offal; it only contains pork butt or shoulder. My grandfather loved it drizzled with sryup for a sweet treat, but I prefer the savory version with salt and pepper! Either way, it immediately brings me back to my childhood.

INGREDIENTS

- 2–2½ lb. pork butt (I prefer bone-in for flavor.)
- 5 cups water or more to fully cover pork butt
- 2 tsp. salt to taste
- 1 tsp. black pepper to taste
- 2 ½ cups finely ground cornmeal
- Crisco or lard

INSTRUCTIONS

1. Place pork in large pot, cover with water, and begin to cook over medium-high heat.
2. Add salt and gently boil until pork falls off bone (2 hours or so).
3. Remove pork and grind through a hand grinder or shred in a stand mixer.
4. Place pork back into water and adjust salt and pepper to taste. Salt liberally because the flavor will become diluted when you add the cornmeal.
5. Whisking briskly, add in cornmeal until mixture is thick enough for a wooden spoon to stand up alone in it.
6. Remove pan from heat and pour into 2 or 3 regular-sized loaf or bread pans.
7. Chill for 3–5 hours.
8. Turn ponhaus out of pan and slice into ¼-inch slices.
9. Fry in Crisco or lard until golden brown and crispy.
10. Serve with eggs and salt and pepper or with syrup.

BASTED EGGS

COOK TIME: 5 Minutes
TOTAL TIME: 10 Minutes
MAKES: 4 Eggs

Basted eggs equal unconditional love to me. My favorite teacher and dear family friend, Mrs. Jullie, would make these for me before school on days when she generously took care of me, even though she had a husband and two small children, along with a full-time teaching job. She would ask what we wanted for breakfast, and once she offered basted eggs and toast, I was hooked and asked for them every time! As I reflect on this as an adult with a family, I was in awe of the love she gave, taking the time to make basted eggs on busy school mornings. I'm forever thankful to Mama Judi Jullie.

INGREDIENTS

- 1 Tbs. butter
- 4 eggs
- 2 Tbs. water
- Salt and pepper

INSTRUCTIONS

1. Heat a 10" nonstick skillet over medium heat, then melt butter in skillet and swirl around.
2. Once butter is melted, crack eggs one at a time and add to the skillet.
3. Allow to cook without moving until the whites are set, about 2 minutes.
4. Add 2 tablespoons of water to the skillet and immediately cover with a lid.
5. Continue to cook until eggs are set but the yolk is still soft, about 2–3 minutes.
6. Remove eggs from the pan immediately so they don't overcook.
7. Season with salt and pepper to taste.

EGG PANCAKES (A.K.A. CREPES)

PREP TIME: 5 Minutes
COOK TIME: 2–3 Minutes
SERVES: 4–6

My grandmother made these almost every Sunday for us in a huge cast-iron pan that stayed on top of her stove. She cut them into quarters and served them with fresh sausage patties. She called them "egg pancakes," describing them as humble farm fare (she grew up with eleven siblings on a small farm). Little did I know, until I was in my 20s and dined at my first European cafe that these were actually fancy French crepes!

INGREDIENTS

- 1 cup all-purpose flour
- 1 tsp. white sugar
- ¼ tsp. salt
- 3 eggs
- 2 cups milk
- 2 Tbs. butter, melted

INSTRUCTIONS

1. Sift together flour, sugar, and salt; set aside. In a large bowl, beat eggs and milk together with an electric mixer. Add flour mixture to egg mixture and beat until smooth; stir in melted butter.

2. Heat a lightly oiled griddle or frying pan over medium-high heat. Pour or scoop the batter onto the griddle, using approximately 2 tablespoons for each crepe.

3. Tip and rotate pan to spread batter as thinly as possible. After about 1½–2 minutes, flip crepe.

4. Lightly brown on other side and serve hot with butter and warm maple syrup or fruit preserves.

STRAWBERRY FREEZER JAM

PREP TIME: 10 Minutes
MAKES: 5 Pint Jars

One of the sure signs of spring was when the sweet, tiny strawberries of Michigan ripened on the vines and my mom, aunts, and grandmother gathered on a Saturday to make freezer jam, sometimes adding rhubarb. It's a sweet memory; nothing was better atop my Aunt Nancy's homemade bread, warm from the oven and slathered with butter. My cousin Carrie has lovingly preserved this tradition with her children.

INGREDIENTS
- 4 cups fresh strawberries, crushed
- 3 cups sugar
- 1.75 ounce package dry pectin
- ¾ cup water
- 1 Tbs. lemon juice

INSTRUCTIONS
1. Mix crushed strawberries with sugar, and let stand for ten minutes. Meanwhile, stir the pectin into the water in a small saucepan. Bring to a boil over medium-high heat and boil for one minute.
2. Stir the boiling water and lemon juice into the strawberries. Allow to stand for 3 minutes before pouring into jars or other storage containers.
3. Place lids on the containers and leave for 24 hours.
4. Store in refrigerator for up to 2 weeks or in freezer for up to 1 year.

HOMEMADE BREAD & STICKY BUNS

PREP TIME: 30–40 Minutes (plus rising and baking time)
MAKES: 5 Loaves Bread or Three Loaves Bread and One Pan Sticky Buns

This homemade bread was eagerly anticipated on Saturday mornings when my Aunt Nancy would drop it off, still warm in a paper bag! After our chores were finished, we would get to toast a slice and slather freezer jam and butter on it. It was such a treat. Sometimes, this delicious bread dough turned into sticky buns on my Grandma and Grandpa's breakfast table.

INGREDIENTS

- 6 Tbs. sugar
- 6 tsp. salt
- 6 Tbs. shortening
- 2 cups water, boiling
- Mix above ingredients together in large bowl. Set aside.
- 1 cup lukewarm water
- 2 pkg yeast (not rapid rise)
- 5 lbs. bread flour or all-purpose flour
- Combine warm water and yeast in small bowl until yeast is dissolved.
- 3 cups cold water

INSTRUCTIONS

1. Add cold water to bowl containing the hot water, shortening, salt, and sugar. Mix until mixture is lukewarm. Add yeast/water mixture and stir until combined.
2. Sift in approximately 5 pounds of flour until dough is kneadable. Knead dough on floured surface for 10 minutes, adding more flour as needed when dough gets sticky.
3. Place dough in large pan or stainless stockpot and cover with a tea towel. Place in a warm place (Aunt Nancy always put it in the oven, not turned on) and let rise for 2 hours. Remove towel and punch dough down. Cover and let rise for 1 hour.
4. Grease bread pans with shortening (the dough will make about 5 loaves of bread or 3 loaves and a 9" x 13" pan or fluted tube pan of sticky buns). Separate dough in 2 balls of dough per loaf pan. Cover pans of dough and let rise for 1 hour.
5. Preheat oven to 375 degrees and bake for about 35–45 minutes. Remove from oven and carefully remove bread from pans. Rub a little shortening on tops of bread (Aunt Nancy always did this).

STICKY BUN VARIATION:

1. If making sticky buns, only make 3 loaves of bread. Take remaining dough and spread out on floured surface. Spread dough with butter, lots of sugar—this is what makes them sticky!—and sprinkle with cinnamon.
2. Roll and tuck dough carefully into a long log. Slice into rolls about 1 ½–2 inches wide. Optional: sprinkle ½–1 cup chopped pecans into the greased pan.
3. Place rolls into greased 9" x 13" or Bundt cake pan and bake along with bread at 375 degrees for 35–40 minutes. They will be done before the bread!
4. Remove from oven and carefully turn pan upside down onto a cooling rack.

FONDUE PARTY

SWISS & CHEDDAR CHEESE FONDUE

PREP TIME: 20 Minutes
SERVES: About 8 as a first course or 4 as a main

Fondue parties were a fun part of our childhood in the '70s. My mom would have a large crowd of family and friends over to sit at long picnic tables and talk, laugh, and eat for hours! She would make the main course of traditional oil fondue with dipping sauces, but I've now added the cheese course and the chocolate dessert course to my parties. I must admit, the cheese course is my favorite.

INGREDIENTS

- 1 ½ Tbs. butter
- 1 Tbs. cornstarch
- ½ tsp. salt
- 1 cup beer or wine
- 1 cup shredded cheddar cheese, shredded (I usually use mild or medium.)
- 1 cup Swiss cheese, shredded
- Dippers for fondue (ham, French bread, apples, potatoes, veggies, etc.)

INSTRUCTIONS

1. Melt the butter over low heat and then add the cornstarch, stirring until well combined. You can use a fondue pot or a saucepan on the stove—either method works great! If you have an electric fondue pot, turn the temperature slightly above warm, as the temperature gets very hot if you go higher than this!
2. Mix the salt in well and then add the beer or wine. Stir continually over medium–low heat until boiling. Continue to stir and boil the mixture for 1 minute.
3. Turn the heat down slightly and then add the cheese.
4. Mix just until the cheese is melted and serve with all of your favorite dippers!

CHOCOLATE FONDUE

PREP TIME: 15 Minutes
COOK TIME: 15 Minutes
SERVES: About 4–6

It was a summer tradition to have fondue parties with a large group of family and friends, and it was always so much fun! However, my mom did not include the chocolate fondue as one of the courses. This has been added to our family tradition ever since I married a chocolate lover! It's as easy and decadent as dessert gets.

INGREDIENTS

- 10–12 oz. semisweet chocolate chips
- ⅔ cup heavy cream
- 1 tsp. pure vanilla extract or almond extract

INSTRUCTIONS

1. In a saucepan, combine the chocolate and cream and heat on low, stirring often until the chocolate is completely melted and the mixture is smooth. Don't let it come to a boil.
2. Once melted, stir in the extract.
3. If needed, stir in heavy cream or milk 1 tablespoon at a time.
4. Pour the mixture into a fondue pot or small slow cooker to keep warm while serving.
5. Serve with dippers of your choice: strawberries, bananas, krispy rice squares, marshmallows, pound cake, angel food cake, or drizzle on Cream Puffs (recipe page 109) for an insanely delicious treat!
6. Chocolate fondue leftovers will keep well in the refrigerator; just reheat on low and enjoy a repeat chocolate fondue experience!

SAFETY TIPS AND ETIQUETTE FOR OIL FONDUE:

1. Take the cooked meats and veggies off the cooking forks and onto your plate with your dinner fork.
2. Use color-coordinated cooking forks to help guests keep track of them.
3. *Never* eat from the cooking fork; doing so could result in dangerous burns and will spread germs if you dip it back into the pot.
4. If other guests already have their cooking forks in the pot, place your cooking fork under theirs. This way, the other guests can get their food out easily.
5. If (I should say when) food falls off a fork into the oil, ask guests to remove their forks from the oil. Remove the fallen item with a slotted spoon, using a pot holder so you don't burn yourself. Then resume your happy fonduing!
6. If oil spatters when first placing food in, turn heat down until the splattering stops. Then turn heat up gradually to the level that is safe and desirable for cooking.

OIL OR BROTH FONDUE

PREP TIME: 30 Minutes
SERVES: 8

One of my fondest childhood memories is having fondue dinners in the summer with family and friends. It's a tradition I've carried on and expanded upon with the addition of the cheese and chocolate courses. My grandmother loved it so much, she would have tunnel vision and only be able to focus on gathering her own food, even with twenty other people at the table. There was never a fondue gathering where we didn't have to stop the action to rescue a runaway potato or tidbit of steak that got away from my grandmother in her excitement over getting to her goodies for dipping. Make sure you reference the fondue etiquette on page 80, "Don't be a Grandma DeBard" at your next party!

INGREDIENTS

- 1–1.5 L. canola oil or other oil with a high smoke point or 1.5 L. beef broth
- Various sauces for dipping; see Suggested Sauces

INSTRUCTIONS

1. Purchase a tender cut of your favorite type of meat. Beef and kielbasa are easy and popular with guests. Chicken, pork, lamb, or seafood are all great. Plan on preparing about half a pound (8 oz.) of raw meat per guest. However, if you are serving other foods such as potatoes, mushrooms, pineapples, etc. or doing all three fondue courses, then plan on about 4 oz. of raw meat per guest.
2. Cut the meat into bite-size slices or cubes. Reserve the cut meat in small bowls for easy serving and refrigerate until needed.
3. Wash and trim the vegetables. We like to use fresh mushrooms and canned whole potatoes, which become crispy and golden when cooked.
4. Refrigerate the raw veggies and pineapple chunks until serving time.
5. Prepare any of the suggested sauces below or purchase good-quality ones and refrigerate until required. Serve in little individual dishes.
6. Heat oil or broth in electric fondue pot to medium high, them turn down as necessary once you start cooking.

SUGGESTED SAUCES:

Ketchup
Whole-grain mustard
Chimichurri sauce
Yum Yum Sauce (recipe on page 31)
Steak Sauce
Teriyaki Sauce

COOKING TIMES:

Steak: 25–30 seconds for rare; 30–35 seconds for medium; 45–60 seconds for well-done
Shrimp: 1–1 ½ minutes
Chicken: 3 minutes
Pineapple: 10–20 seconds
Potatoes: 2–3 minutes
Mushrooms: 30–35 seconds
Kielbasa: 30–45 seconds

CREAM PUFFS (A.K.A. PATE A CHOUX)

MAKES: 1 dozen (small) or 8 (large)
PREP TIME: 20 Minutes
COOK TIME: 20–25 Minutes

I knew them simply as cream puffs, and it was a sure sign that company was coming (Aunt Ruth and Uncle Forrie) when I saw my mom adding eggs to that batter on the stove. This is a great recipe to make ahead to use with sweet or savory fillings as well as an impressive dessert or appetizer. This also makes an elegant dessert served with chocolate fondue (recipe page 105).

INGREDIENTS

- ½ cup (1 stick) unsalted butter, cut into 8 pieces
- ½ cup water
- ½ cup whole milk
- ¼ tsp. salt
- 2 tsp. granulated sugar
- 1 cup all-purpose flour, spooned into cup and leveled
- 5 large eggs, beaten

INSTRUCTIONS

1. Preheat oven to 400 degrees.
2. In a medium saucepan, combine butter, water, milk, salt, and granulated sugar over medium heat. Stir until the butter has melted. Bring mixture to a simmer, then reduce heat to low and add the flour all at one time. Stir vigorously and continually for 1 minute until lumps smooth out, pressing dough out to sides and bottom of saucepan, as this will cook the flour taste out. Stir until smooth and supple. Then turn off heat.
3. Place dough in bowl of stand mixer and let cool for about 10 minutes, then add eggs, very little at a time, mixing on low speed. Keep mixing on low speed while adding eggs; the dough will start out looking curdled but don't worry! It will eventually come together and be smooth, shiny, and ready for piping.
4. Reserve just a bit of the egg mixture to brush on the puffs before baking.
5. The dough can be refrigerated up to 4 days or frozen for up to 1 month at this point.
6. If you want to bake the cream pufffs now, line a baking sheet with parchment and lightly spray with water (this will create steam which will add moisture to the dough and create a hollow inside for filling).
7. Fill either a sturdy plastic sandwich bag or a piping bag with dough. Cut about 2 inches off the corner and pipe round puffs (2–3 inches in diameter) or rectangular puffs (for eclairs). Place on baking sheet about 3 inches apart. Brush lightly with reserved beaten egg, adding a drop or two of water if too thick.
8. Bake into 400-degree oven for 20–25 minutes until golden brown and puffed!
9. Cool on a rack. Using a chopstick, gently make a hole on the side or end. Fill with whipped cream, Chantilly cream, or custard and drizzle with chocolate sauce (see recipe for Grandma's DeBard's Chocolate Sauce, page 34).

ALL-AMERICAN SUMMER

CHICKEN SALAD

PREP TIME: 15 Minutes
MAKES: 6 Cups

My mom did some catering to supplement her income. I used to tease her that she had just two menus to choose from and both contained chicken salad croissants. Her recipe is very basic but always tasty. After years of menu planning for client events, I find that it's true for me as well; people just love chicken salad. A few upgrades or additions add crunch, texture and taste.

INGREDIENTS

- 4 cups cooked chicken (4 medium boneless breasts or 1 large rotisserie chicken), cubed or shredded **
- 1 cup mayonnaise (Tutu used Hellmann's.)
- 2 Tbs. Dijon mustard
- 2 stalks celery, diced
- ¼–½ cup grated or finely minced sweet onion
- ¼ cup rcd bell pepper, diced (my addition)
- ¼ cup dried cranberries or cherries, slightly chopped
- 1–2 tsp. thyme, tarragon or favorite dried herb
- Lawry's Seasoned Salt and pepper to taste
- ½ tsp. paprika

OPTIONAL:
- ½ cup chopped nuts
- ¼ cup crushed pineapple, drained (a favorite of my BFF)
- ¼ cup red or green grapes, quartered

INSTRUCTIONS

1. Bake or boil chicken breasts if using uncooked chicken. I like to bake covered with lemon, salt, and pepper at 350 degrees for 20–30 minutes.
2. If using rotisserie chicken, remove meat and set aside skin and bones for making stock if desired. Place warm chicken in bowl of KitchenAid mixer and give it a few whirls with the large paddle attachment; the chicken will shred beautifully and easily.
3. Prep and mix all other ingredients in a large bowl. Add chicken and blend gently.

> **TIP**
> Serve on croissants or a nice bed of mixed greens, add to a snack or charcuterie platter with your favorite crackers, or make small tea sandwiches on crustless bread.

SEVEN LAYER SALAD

PREP TIME: 15-20 Minutes
CHILL TIME: 8–24 Hours
SERVES: 8–12

Flashback to the coolest potluck dish of the '70s; I used to seek it out at church functions and parties. The ability to make this salad ahead of time, with the dressing on top and all the veggies staying crisp and fresh underneath, is so convenient, making it the perfect choice to tote along to parties!

INGREDIENTS

- 1 head iceberg or romaine lettuce
- ½ cup red onion, diced
- 1 cup (2–3 stalks) celery, sliced
- 1 red bell pepper, diced
- 12 oz. frozen peas, rinsed and thawed
- 1 cup mayonnaise
- 1 Tbs. sugar (optional)
- 1 packet ranch dressing (optional)
- 1 cup cheddar cheese, shredded
- ½ lb. bacon, fried crisp and crumbled, or a 3 oz. bag of real bacon pieces

INSTRUCTIONS

1. Rinse and prepare vegetables. Set aside.
2. Rinse frozen peas in colander. Set aside.
3. If using uncooked bacon, fry and set aside.
4. Mix mayonnaise, sugar, and ranch dressing packet. Set aside.
5. In 9" x 13" dish or glass trifle bowl, layer evenly: lettuce, red onion, celery, red pepper, and peas.
6. Carefully spread mayonnaise dressing mixture over peas.
7. Sprinkle cheese and bacon over top and cover tightly with lid or plastic wrap and refrigerate.
8. Chill for up to 24 hours before serving.

COOLER CORN

PREP TIME: 15 Minutes
COOK TIME: 30 Minutes

Summer sweet corn is a delight we looked forward to all winter long in Michigan. No summer cookout is complete without this fresh, snappy vegetable that's most fun to eat right off the cob! This recipe makes easy, portable corn (with wooden holding sticks and jars of melted butter for dipping); perfect for a self-serve bar at your picnic or pool party!

INGREDIENTS

- *Clean* cooler, any size works (don't use foam)
- 8–12 ears of fresh corn (or more, depending on the size of your cooler)
- Boiling water (about 2 qts. per 12 ears of corn)
- Kosher salt
- Butter, melted
- Favorite dried herbs and spices
- Wooden sticks or skewers

INSTRUCTIONS

1. Shuck all the corn and rinse thoroughly.
2. Place the shucked corn inside the clean cooler. It doesn't matter how you put it in as long as the water covers it.
3. Boil the water. Make sure the water is at a full boil before you pour it in.
4. Add water to cover all pieces of corn. Sprinkle a few teaspoons of salt and 1 tablespoon of sugar into water. Snap down the lid and let stand for 30 minutes.
5. Serve with wooden sticks for holding, melted butter in a jar for dipping, and your favorite herbs and spices for sprinkling on or rolling the corn into.
6. Enjoy! With the lid on, the corn should stay hot for about 2 hours.

BANANA WHIPPED CREAM CAKE

PREP TIME: 10–15 Minutes
COOK TIME: 28–33 Minutes
SERVES: 8–10

This simple and semi-homemade cake has put a smile on many faces over the years. It was one of the top two birthday cakes my mom made for teachers and dear friends and relatives (The other one was her Raspberry Whipped Cream Angel Food Cake; see recipe on page 121.) It was also my Uncle Dan's favorite, and he remembers it to this day. I still have the Tupperware cake carrier that she used to deliver them.

INGREDIENTS

- 15.25 oz. yellow cake mix (I like Duncan Hines.)
- 4 large eggs
- ⅓ cup butter, melted
- 1 cup whole milk
- A few Tbs. lemon juice or banana liqueur (to prevent banana slices from turning brown)
- 3 firm bananas (barely ripe), sliced
- 1 pt. heavy whipping cream
- 4–5 Tbs. powdered sugar
- 1 Tbs. vanilla extract or inside of 1 vanilla bean

INSTRUCTIONS FOR ICING

1. Using chilled bowl and beaters, start beating whipping cream on low speed, increasing the speed as it thickens.
2. Beat until fairly stiff peaks form. Add powdered sugar and vanilla extract and beat on low until just incorporated.

INSTRUCTIONS FOR FILLING

1. Toss banana slices with the lemon juice or liqueur.

INSTRUCTIONS FOR CAKE

1. Bake cake as directed but substitute milk for water, melted butter for vegetable oil, and 4 eggs for 3 eggs. Bake in two 8" or 9" round pans and cool completely.
2. Carefully slice each cake in half horizontally.
3. Place one layer of banana slices between each of three layers, leaving top empty.
4. Frost sides and top of cake.
5. Cover and refrigerate. Enjoy within 24 hours for best appearance and flavor.

RASPBERRY WHIPPED CREAM ANGEL FOOD CAKE

PREP TIME: 5–10 Minutes
COOK TIME: 38–48
SERVES: 8–10

This is another boxed cake lovingly made by my mom for teachers, family, and friends. Many a birthday has been celebrated with this light, fresh, and super-simple summer cake. I always knew when I came home and saw one of these cakes resting upside down on coffee cups on the kitchen counter that someone was getting a cake for their special day!

INGREDIENTS

- 1 box Angel food cake mix
- 1 ⅓ cups water
- 1 pt. heavy whipping cream
- 4–5 Tbs. powdered sugar
- 1 Tbs. vanilla extract or inside of 1 vanilla bean
- 2 pts. fresh raspberries or 1 bag frozen raspberries, thawed and rinsed

INSTRUCTIONS

1. Move oven rack to lowest position (and remove other racks) if using angel food pan or to middle position if using loaf pans. Heat oven to 350 degrees if using a shiny metal pan or 325 degrees if using a nonstick pan. **Do not grease pan**.

2. Beat cake mix and water in extra-large glass or metal bowl on low speed for 30 seconds; beat on medium speed for 1 minute. Pour into an ungreased pan. (Do not use Bundt® pan or angel food pan that is smaller than 10" x 4" because batter will overflow.)

3. Bake as directed or until top is dark golden brown and cracks feel very dry and not sticky. **Do not underbake.**

4. Immediately turn pan upside down onto glass bottle or rest each of its 3 prongs onto upside-down coffee cups until cake is completely cool. Run knife around edges; remove from pan.

5. Using chilled bowl and beaters, start beating whipping cream on low speed, increasing the speed as it thickens.

6. Beat until fairly stiff peaks form and then add powdered sugar and vanilla extract and beat on low until just incorporated. If using frozen raspberries, fold in at this point.

7. Then top cooled cake with whipped cream and fresh raspberries. Refrigerate immediately and enjoy within 24 hours for best taste!

> **TIP**
> Cut cake with serrated knife, using sawing motion, or with electric knife. Store tightly covered.

FRESHLY SQUEEZED LEMONADE

PREP TIME: 30 Minutes
SERVES: 10 (8-ounce glasses)

Diet Coke may have been Tutu's go-to beverage, but she couldn't resist that tart, cool flavor of freshly squeezed lemonade at a summer fair or amusement park. This very straightforward recipe will quench your thirst on a hot summer day. Try the blueberry or peach simple syrup option for a special occasion or when the blueberry or peach harvest is at its peak!

INGREDIENTS

- 2 cups fresh lemon juice (zest first and include zest for additional tartness). Depending on the size of the lemons, 8–12 of them should be enough for two cups of juice.
- 2 cups sugar
- 8–10 cups water

INSTRUCTIONS

Make simple syrup:

1. Place the sugar and water in a small saucepan and bring to a simmer. Stir so that the sugar dissolves completely and remove from heat. (**Option:** Add two cups of fresh blueberries or peaches when in season, then strain fruit out of the simple syrup.)

Juice the lemons:

1. While the water is heating for the simple syrup, juice the lemons.
2. Combine lemon juice, simple syrup and water (if using zest, add at this time.)
3. Pour the mixture into a serving pitcher. Add 4–6 cups of cold water and taste. Add more water if you would like it to be more diluted (though note that when you add ice, it will melt and naturally dilute the lemonade).

Chill:

1. Refrigerate 30–40 minutes. Serve with ice and sliced lemons. (Or garnish with fresh blueberries or peaches if opting for blueberry or peach lemonade variations.)

SEAFOOD BOIL

PERFECT ICED TEA

PREP TIME: 5 Minutes
BREW TIME: 15 Minutes
MAKES: 2 Quarts

In Michigan, a request for "sweet tea" would probably cause someone to point to the sugar bowl or sweeteners for you to add as desired. After living in the South for over thirty years, I am now fully versed in the terms "sweet" and "unsweet" tea!

INGREDIENTS

- 1 pinch baking soda
- 2 cups boiling water
- 6 of your favorite individual tea bags (I use black pekoe.)
- ¾–1 ½ cups sugar (optional, except in the South)
- 6 cups cool water
- Lemon wedges and fresh mint (optional)

INSTRUCTIONS

1. Boil 2 cups water. Add baking soda and tea bags to a heat-resistant pitcher or jar. Pour boiling water over and cover. Set aside to steep for 15 minutes.

2. Remove tea bags (do not squeeze) and add sugar, if desired. Stir to dissolve sugar. Add the cool water.

3. Chill and serve over ice with lemon and mint if desired.

TIP

Baking soda counteracts the tannins in tea which eliminates the bitterness. It also makes sweet tea appear less cloudy.

SUMMER SHRIMP AND AVOCADO "SALSA"

PREP TIME: 5–10 Minutes
MARINATING TIME: 2–6 hours
SERVES: 8

My client (and now dear friend), Stacey, shared this recipe with me, and now it's a permanent part of my client menus when I am a vacation chef. Scrumptious, fresh and oh, so simple!

INGREDIENTS

- 1 red onion
- 2–3 plum tomatoes
- 2 lbs. shrimp, peeled, deveined, and cooked (chopped if large)
- 2 cups ketchup
- 2 Tbs. hot sauce (I use Texas Pete.)
- 2 Tbs. lime juice
- Fresh cilantro (small bunch, about ¼ cup)
- 2 avocados

INSTRUCTIONS

1. Dice red onion. Chop tomatoes.
2. Add shrimp and cut into bite-size pieces.
3. Mix ketchup, hot sauce, and lime juice. Pour over shrimp mixture.
4. Add chopped cilantro or other fresh herb of your choice.
5. Marinate for 2–6 hours.
6. Add two diced avocados just before serving.
7. Serve with tortilla chips

CUCUMBER SALAD

PREP TIME: 10 Minutes
MARINATE TIME: 1–3 Hours
SERVES: 8

Summertime in Michigan means a bountiful harvest of cucumbers! This simple salad was on the table routinely at my Aunt Jan and Uncle Vic's house on those fun-filled vacations with my cousins and the promise of a swim in the lake after dinner. Quick, simple, and perfect for those humid days.

INGREDIENTS

- 2 large cucumbers, washed, partially peeled, and thinly sliced
- 1 sweet onion, thinly sliced (I love Vidalia onions.)
- 1 Tbs. sea salt
- 1 tsp. ground white pepper or freshly cracked black pepper
- 1 tsp. garlic powder
- 1 tsp. dried dill or 1 Tbs. fresh dill
- 2 Tbs. vinegar apple cider vinegar, white vinegar, or champagne vinegar
- ½ cup mayonnaise
- ½ cup sour cream
- 1 Tbs. sugar (optional, except in the South)

INSTRUCTIONS

1. Mix cucumbers, sweet onion, and sea salt together in a bowl. Cover bowl with plastic wrap and let sit for 30 minutes.
2. Turn cucumber mixture into a colander set over a bowl or in a sink; let drain, stirring occasionally, until most of the liquid has drained. Transfer drained cucumber mixture to a large bowl.
3. Whisk mayonnaise, sour cream, vinegar, sugar, dill, garlic powder, and pepper together in a bowl until smooth; pour over the cucumber mixture and stir to coat.
4. For best flavor, marinate in refrigerator for 1–3 hours. (I usually can't wait that long!)

LOW COUNTRY SEAFOOD BOIL

PREP TIME: 15 Minutes
COOK TIME: 25–35 Minutes
MAKES: 12–14

The availability of fresh coastal shrimp is scarce around the Great Lakes, but after I moved to the Carolinas in 1986, I started enjoying the mother lode of fresh shellfish and was hooked on this fresh seafood tradition that varies regionally (e.g., the clambake of Rhode Island, where my sister-in-law Kathleen grew up, or the smelt dip or perch fry of Michigan). A seafood boil is the perfect casual gathering for celebrating with friends and enjoying local seafood. It has turned into a birthday tradition for my daughter, Taylor, and a client favorite for my summer vacationers.

INGREDIENTS

- 1–3 Tbs. seafood seasoning such as Old Bay® to taste
- 1 stick butter
- 2 lemons, halved
- 1 large sweet onion, halved
- 5 lbs. small new potatoes
- 3 (16 oz.) packages cooked kielbasa sausage, cut into 1-inch pieces
- 8 ears fresh corn cut into thirds, husks and silk removed
- 5–6 lbs. (or more) snow crab legs
- 3–4 lbs. fresh shrimp, deveined with peel on

INSTRUCTIONS

1. Add water to a large pot with a tight-fitting lid (and built-in strainer, if possible), filling ⅓ of the way. Place over an outdoor cooker or indoors on medium-high heat.
2. Add butter and Old Bay seasoning to taste and bring to a full boil. Add potatoes and onion; cover and cook for 15 minutes.
3. Add corn, sausage, crab legs, and lemons; cook for 5 minutes.
4. Add shrimp when everything else is almost done, cooking for another 3–5 minutes until the shrimp turns pink.
5. Meanwhile, cover a picnic table with a disposable plastic tablecloth. Cover tablecloth with newspapers or brown kraft paper down the center. Provide plenty of napkins, cocktail sauce, melted butter, lemon wedges, cold beer, soda, and sweet tea!
6. Drain shrimp and pour them onto the table.
7. Great served with cornbread and key lime pie for dessert!

WATERMELON SALAD

PREP TIME: 15 Minutes
SERVES: 4–8

My mom and grandfather *loved* watermelon! Many a time when I visited my grandparents' house, I found my grandpa at the kitchen table with a slice of juicy watermelon and the salt shaker. He always told me that salting it enhanced the flavor. This watermelon salad does the same with the addition of the salty feta and the briny olives.

INGREDIENTS

- 1 cup sliced red onion
- 3 Tbs. red wine vinegar
- 1 Tbs. sugar
- ¼ tsp. kosher salt
- 2 tsp. extra-virgin olive oil
- 2 cups watermelon, cubed
- 1 oz. (about ¼ cup) feta, crumbled
- ½ cup baby arugula
- 2 Tbs. Kalamata olives, coarsely chopped
- 2 Tbs. small mint leaves, torn
- ½ Tbs. balsamic glaze (optional)

INSTRUCTIONS

1. Cut watermelon into bite-size chunks.
2. Combine onion, vinegar, sugar, and salt in a medium bowl; let stand 15 minutes or until onion is softened, tossing occasionally.
3. Top watermelon evenly with onions, feta, arugula, olives, leftover vinegar mixture (I don't use all of it).
4. Sprinkle with mint and drizzle with balsamic glaze (optional).
5. Toss and serve immediately!

TUTU'S TATER SALAD

PREP TIME: About 30 Minutes
SERVES: 8–12

No summer supper was complete without Tutu's Tater Salad, and no bowl was served without the addition of chopped hard-boiled eggs. This creamy, savory and slightly tangy recipe is pure American comfort! Feel free to change or add seasoning according to your taste.

INGREDIENTS

- 3 lbs. (5–6 medium) red potatoes, washed and cut into 1" cubes
- 1 cup Hellmann's mayonnaise
- 2 Tbs. vinegar
- 1 Tbs. yellow mustard
- 2 tsp. seasoned salt
- ¼–½ tsp. ground black pepper
- 1 cup celery, diced (or more to taste)
- ½ cup sweet onion, diced
- 1 Tbs. fresh parsley or dill
- 4 hard-boiled eggs, chopped

INSTRUCTIONS

1. Cover potatoes with water in 4-quart saucepan; bring to a boil over medium-high heat. Reduce heat and simmer until potatoes are tender, about 10 minutes. Drain and cool slightly.
2. Combine mayonnaise, vinegar, mustard, parsley, salt, and pepper in large bowl. Add potatoes and remaining ingredients and toss gently. Serve chilled or at room temperature.
3. Make sure to toss potatoes with the dressing while they are still warm.

CLASSIC PIMENTO CHEESE

PREP TIME: 10 Minutes
MAKES: 2–2 ½ cups

I moved to the Carolinas in the late '80s and was introduced to this simple and classic Southern staple. I've been hooked ever since! Nothing says hospitality like a creamy bowl of pimento cheese with crackers ... on the porch with neighbors, good conversation, and a cold beverage!

INGREDIENTS

- 2 cups extra-sharp cheddar cheese, shredded
- 1–1 ½ cups mayonnaise (Duke's is recommended)
- ¼ tsp. garlic powder
- 1 tsp. dried chives
- ¼ tsp. ground cayenne pepper or hot sauce
- ½ teaspoon Worcestershire sauce (Just a shake will do.)
- 4 oz. jar diced pimentos, drained

INSTRUCTIONS

1. Mix all ingredients thoroughly (but gently) so that everything is incorporated. Taste and adjust seasoning according to your taste.
2. Chill. Serve with crackers, crudités, or French rounds. (Pimento cheese is also good on a burger or in a grilled cheese sandwich.)

THANKSGIVING FEAST

UPSIDE DOWN ROAST TURKEY

PREP TIME: 10–15 Minutes (plus thaw time)
COOK TIME: 3 ½ Hours (Depending on size)
SERVES: 6–8 (for 12–15 pound bird)

No one made a juicier, more tender turkey than my mom! Her insistence that it be roasted upside down (breast down) ensured that all the juices ran into the breast and kept it from drying out. She could never carve it at the table because it literally fell of the bone! Many turkey-loving converts were born after tasting this jucy, flavorful recipe and roasting method.

INGREDIENTS

- 12–15 lb. turkey (Adjust seasonings and aromatics for larger turkey.)
- ½ stick butter or olive oil
- 2 Tbs. flour (if using the roasting bag)
- 3 Tbs. Lawry's Seasoned Salt
- 1 Tbs. cracked black pepper
- 1 medium onion, cored and quartered
- 2 stalks celery
- 1 whole carrot with fronds attached
- 1 small apple, quartered and core removed
- 1 orange, quartered
- 6 sprigs fresh thyme
- 4 sprigs fresh rosemary

INSTRUCTIONS

1. If using a frozen turkey, thaw in the refrigerator, allowing 1 day of thawing for every 4 pounds.
2. Remove the giblets and neck from inside the turkey's cavity and set aside.
3. Set the turkey on a roasting rack set inside a roasting pan. Melt butter and brush turkey inside and out with butter. Sprinkle the turkey inside and out with salt and pepper. Place the onion, celery, apple, orange, and herbs in the cavity of the turkey. Place the turkey breast-side down on the roasting rack *or* slip it into a roasting bag and add flour. Shake flour around carefully and close bag, then place into roasting pan, breast-side down.
4. Roast the turkey. Arrange a rack in the middle of the oven, remove any racks above it, and preheat to 400 degrees. Roast the turkey for 30 minutes to darken and crisp the skin. Reduce the heat to 300 degrees and roast the bird for 1 hour *per* every 4 pounds (e.g., 12 pounds = 3 hours, 16 pounds = 4 hours, etc.).
5. Finish the turkey. Begin checking the temperature of the turkey after 2 hours of roasting at 300 degrees.
6. Use a probe thermometer to check the turkey's temperature in both the thighs and the breast. The turkey is ready when it registers 165 degrees for the thighs and 160 degrees for the breasts.
7. Rest and carve. Remove the turkey from the oven and let rest for 15–20 minutes before carving. (If it turns out like Tutu's, there will be no carving necessary because it will fall apart and be *so* tender and juicy.)

STRAWBERRY PRETZEL SALAD

PREP TIME: 15 Minutes
SERVES: 8–12

My dear friend Ellen made this for a neighborhood gathering, and though I don't love Jell-O, strawberries, or pretzels, I fell in love with this combination of sweet, salty, smooth, and crunchy. Jell-O "salads" were a part of every family celebration when I was growing up, and I'm certain this recipe will help me continue that tradition! I've added a cranberry variation as an option for a delicious Thanksgiving dish.

INGREDIENTS

- 2 cups pretzels, crushed
- ¾ cup butter, melted
- 3 Tbs. white sugar for the crust
- 8 oz. package cream cheese, softened
- 1 cup white sugar for the cream cheese layer
- 8 oz. container frozen whipped topping, thawed
- 2 (3 oz.) packages strawberry flavored Jell-O or cherry Jell-O if making the cranberry vresion
- 2 cups boiling water
- 2 10 oz. packages frozen strawberries or 20 oz. fresh strawberries or 2 cans whole cranberry sauce, chilled

INSTRUCTIONS

1. Preheat oven to 400 degrees.
2. Stir together crushed pretzels, melted butter, and 3 tablespoons sugar; mix well and press mixture into the bottom of a 9" x 13" baking dish.
3. Bake 8–10 minutes until set. Set aside to cool.
4. In a large mixing bowl, cream together cream cheese and 1 cup sugar. Fold in whipped topping. Spread mixture onto cooled crust.
5. Dissolve Jell-O in boiling water. Stir in frozen strawberries, fresh strawberries, or cranberry sauce and allow to set briefly. When mixture is about the consistency of egg whites, pour and spread over cream cheese layer. Refrigerate until set.

EASY-PEASY MACARONI & CHEESE

PREP TIME: 10 Minutes
TOTAL TIME: 1 Hour 10 Minutes
SERVES: 8

This recipe makes life easier because you don't have to cook the macaroni before you bake it! Growing up, boxed Kraft was our staple, but my mom baked it in the oven with added cheese. It was an economical and filling dinner served with applesauce, green beans, and blueberry muffins to satisfy four children. This recipe is a keeper and has many optional additions, with lobster being my personal favorite.

INGREDIENTS

- 3 Tbs. butter
- 2 ½ cups (½ lb.) uncooked macaroni
- 1 tsp. salt
- 1 pinch black pepper
- 1 pinch cayenne pepper
- ½ tsp. smoked paprika
- Pinch of ground dry mustard and dash of Worcestershire sauce (optional)
- 3 cups sharp cheddar, extra-sharp cheddar, or any cheese, shredded
- 1 lb. Velveeta, cubed
- 4 ½ cups whole milk

INSTRUCTIONS

1. Preheat oven to 350 degrees.
2. Place butter in a 9" x 13" dish. Place dish in hot oven until butter melts.
3. Remove dish and tilt, fully coating the bottom and slightly coating the sides with melted butter.
4. Add dry macaroni and spices and stir to coat.
5. Sprinkle with cheese and Velveeta cubes.
6. Pour milk over evenly. *Do not stir*! (You can press down slightly to submerge macaroni fully.)
7. Bake uncovered for one hour.

TIP
Prior to baking, consider these recipe-enhancing add-ins: diced ham or bacon, petite peas or frozen peas, broccoli, crabmeat, shrimp or lobster, pulled pork or pulled rotisserie chicken, pimentos or sliced olives, broccoli, cauliflower or sautéed mushrooms, or diced jalapeños.

SWEET POTATO CASSEROLE

PREP TIME: 15–20 Minutes
COOK TIME: 30–40 Minutes
SERVES: 10–12

Wanda, our precious neighbor—who happens to be an incredibly talented cook—shared this recipe with me years ago, and it has become a favorite side dish at our Thanksgiving table. It is decadent and full of traditional Southern flavor!

INGREDIENTS

- 5 cups fresh sweet potatoes
- ½ cup butter, melted
- 1 cup sugar
- 1 tsp. pure vanilla extract
- 1 tsp. cinnamon
- Pinch of salt

TOPPING

- 1 cup brown sugar
- ½ cup flour
- ½–1 tsp. cinnamon
- ⅓ cup melted butter
- ½ cup pecans, chopped

INSTRUCTIONS

1. Cut potatoes in half (no need to peel) and boil in salted water until fork-tender (about 20 minutes). Drain and when cool enough, slip out of peels and mash well.

2. Mix the mashed potatoes with other ingredients: butter, sugar, vanilla, cinnamon and salt (not topping ingredients) and put into greased 9" x 13" pan.

3. Mix all topping ingredients. Spread evenly and gently over the top of potato mixture.

4. Cover and bake at 350 degrees for 30–40 minutes, then uncover and bake for additional 10 minutes.

WILD RICE AND SAUSAGE CASSEROLE

PREP TIME: 20 Minutes
COOK TIME: 60–90 Minutes
SERVES: 8–10

Discovered by my beloved sister-in-law Kathleen many years ago in the *Charlotte Observer*, this recipe became my brother's most requested side dish for Thanksgiving. My daughter, Taylor, has now taken the reigns in making this dish for holidays and for her staff work parties. It is a wonderful complement to turkey, as well as pork roast or roasted chicken.

INGREDIENTS

- 16 oz. package ground pork sausage
- (3–4 stalks) celery, chopped
- 1 large onion, chopped
- 1 medium green pepper, seeded and chopped
- 1 clove garlic, minced
- 2 (14.5 oz.) cans chicken broth
- 10.25 oz. can cream of mushroom soup
- 10.25 oz. can cream of chicken soup
- 8 oz. can of water chestnuts, drained
- 2 4 oz. cans sliced mushrooms, drained
- 6 oz. package long grain and wild rice mix
- ½–1 tsp. dried thyme
- ¼ cup sliced or slivered almonds
- Fresh parsley (optional)

INSTRUCTIONS

1. Combine sausage, celery, onion, green pepper, and garlic in large skillet and cook over medium heat until sausage is browned and vegetables are tender, stirring until meat crumbles.
2. Drain if necessary.
3. Stir in chicken broth, mushroom soup, chicken soup, water chestnuts, mushrooms, rice mix, and thyme. Spoon mixture into a lightly greased 3-quart baking dish. Sprinkle with almonds. Bake uncovered at 350 degrees for 60–90 minutes.
4. Let stand five minutes before serving.
5. Garnish with fresh parsley if desired.

GLAZE

- 1 cup Confectioners sugar
- 2 Tbsp. Half & Half or whole milk (enough to make smooth, thick glaze)
- 1 tsp. almond or vanilla extract (optional)

1. While baking, mix together ingredients for the glaze and set aside.
2. Remove pies from the oven and allow to cool on the pan until ready to handle. Drizzle with glaze and serve slightly warm.

GLAZED CHERRY HAND PIES

PREP TIME: 25 Minutes
COOK TIME: 30-35 Minutes
MAKES: 18-24 Hand pies (depending upon size)

There are no better cherries for baking than those grown in the Traverse City area of Michigan. I love the tart flavor that makes your cheeks pucker. Having your own pie is a special treat for the holidays or anytime.

INGREDIENTS

For the Pie Filling:

- 1 ½ Tbsp. cornstarch
- 1 ½ Tbsp. cold water
- 5 cups frozen tart cherries or fresh tart cherries, pitted
- ½ cup granulated sugar
- 1 Tbsp. lemon juice
- ⅛ teaspoon salt
- 1 teaspoon pure almond extract
- 2 packages pie crust dough or 24 GOYA empanada discs
- 1 egg, beaten, for brushing
- Granulated sugar, for garnish

INSTRUCTIONS

1. Mix the cornstarch and water together in a small bowl until combined and milky. Set aside.
2. In a medium saucepan, combine the cherries, sugar, lemon juice, and salt. Stirring occasionally with a rubber spatula or wooden spoon, cook over medium heat until the cherries begin to release their juices, about 5 minutes.
3. Stir in the cornstarch mixture, then bring to a boil while stirring often. Once boiling, remove from heat then stir in the almond extract
4. Allow to cool completely at room temperature.
5. Preheat oven to 375 degrees
6. Line 2 large baking sheets with parchment paper or a silicone baking mat.
7. On a lightly floured surface, lay out one pie crust or about 6 empanada discs (don't put all out at once or they will dry out. Roll out just slightly and cut 4 inch circles (I use a plastic pie cutter and crimper specifically made for this.) Brush the edges of the bottom rectangles with the egg wash. Spoon 2-3 Tbsp. of cooled cherry mixture onto each of the bottom circles/discs. Fold in half and crimp edges to seal over the cherry filling, lining up the edges as best you can. Crimp the edges with a fork to seal shut if not using the cutter. Repeat this entire step with all dough. Slice 2-3 slits in the tops for air vents.
8. Brush the tops of the pies with egg wash, then sprinkle with granulated sugar.
9. Bake the pastry pies for 30-35 minutes, or until the tops are golden brown. Make sure to rotate the baking sheet once during bake time.

> **TIP**
> The filling can be made up to 5 days in advance and stored in the refrigerator. I like to do this several days before Thanksgiving to make things a bit less hectic. Tutu would approve, as she was always very organized!

MINCEMEAT TART

PREP TIME: 10 Minutes (if using jarred mincemeat or 40 minutes if making homemade)
COOK TIME: 30 Minutes
SERVES: 10

The word "mincemeat" is not very attractive in terms of marketing, but the modern version made with fall fruit, citrus zest, and spices, plus nuts to make it more decadent, is truly delicious, and it was a favorite of my sister Barb's and a few of my aunts. It was traditionally served in pie form for us at Thanksgiving, but I like it in tart form because then you don't have too much crust disguising the robust flavors. Serve it with a scoop of vanilla ice cream for a perfect fall treat.

INGREDIENTS

- 1 27 oz. jar None Such Mincemeat (for quick version) OR

Homemade Mincemeat:

- 3 apples or pears or a mixture of both, unpeeled (Chop half of the fruit and coarsely grate the other half.)
- 1 lemon (zest and juice only)
- 1 orange (zest and juice only)
- 1 cup golden or regular raisins
- 1 cup currants
- 1 cup packed brown sugar
- ½ cup orange juice, brandy, rum, or water (I like brandy.)
- 1–2 cinnamon sticks
- 1 tsp. pumpkin pie spice
- Pinch of salt
- ½ cup walnuts or pecans, chopped and toasted for added flavor
- ¼ cup butter, grated, or ¼ cup ghee (for vegan mincemeat)
- Piecrust (I use tried and true Pillsbury piecrust.)

INSTRUCTIONS

1. In a large saucepan, combine all the ingredients except the butter and nuts. Bring to a simmer and cook, stirring often, for 20–30 minutes until dark golden and thick.
2. Mixture should be thick and slightly saucy. If it looks dry, add a little more liquid.
3. Remove from the heat and let cool; stir in the grated butter or ghee and the nuts if using them.
4. Store in clean, sealed mason jars for up to 2 weeks in the refrigerator or up to 6 months in the freezer.
5. Line a tart pan with piecrust. Pierce with a fork and blind-bake for about 10 minutes. Add filling (homemade or jarred) and bake according to package directions for one pie. Use excess piecrust to create decorations for the top (optional).
6. Let cool on wire rack and remove from tart pan carefully. (You can leave bottom of tart pan on to make it easier to slice.)
7. Enjoy warmed with a scoop of vanilla ice cream and a steaming hot cup of coffee!

CHRISTMAS DINNER

PERK-A-PUNCH

PREP TIME: 5 Minutes
PERK TIME: 30 Minutes
MAKES: 5 quarts

In my early twenties, my darling roommate, Jodi, shared this family recipe with me. I used it for my first ever catering menu, and everyone loved its fragrant holiday spices. It warms your tummy and is a special holiday beverage from Thanksgiving to Christmas and through New Year's Day! (I refrigerate it between gatherings and then return it to the percolator to make the house smell incredible!)

INGREDIENTS

- 2 qts. cranberry juice
- 2 qts. pineapple juice
- 1 qt. water
- ⅔ cup brown sugar
- 1 Tbs. whole cloves
- 1 Tbs. whole allspice
- 4 cinnamon sticks
- 1 orange, sliced
- ½ lemon, sliced

INSTRUCTIONS

1. Place juices in the bottom of a 30-cup percolator.
2. Set basket in place, then put remaining ingredients in basket.
3. Perk 30 minutes or until the light signals brewing is complete.

Optional: Garnish with cinnamon sticks or whole cranberries.

COLD COFFEE PUNCH

PREP TIME: 10–15 Minutes
MAKES: 16-20 cups

This recipe was given to me by Pat, the aunt of my daughter's college boyfriend. It was served at a small church wedding as a nonalcoholic punch, and its creamy coffee taste was addicting! It has been a favorite for my "Girls' Annual Holiday Brunch" (with the option of a bourbon or rum addition) for years.

INGREDIENTS

- 1 gallon of whole milk (must use whole)
- ½ gallon of vanilla ice cream
- ½ gallon of chocolate ice cream
- 2 oz. instant coffee (can use decaf)
- 2 cups of sugar
- 1 cup of water

INSTRUCTIONS

1. In a saucepan, mix the coffee, sugar, and water and heat until melted.
2. Refrigerate coffee mixture. The liquid will get syrupy.
3. Before guests arrive, pour chilled syrup in punch bowl.
4. Add entire gallon of milk.
5. Add all the ice cream (by scoopfuls) into the punch.
6. Stir.
7. The ice cream doesn't have to melt all the way—it serves as the ice.
8. I add very cold bourbon or rum to taste.

HOT SPINACH AND ARTICHOKE DIP

PREP TIME: 5 Minutes
COOK TIME: 30 Minutes
SERVES: 8

Hot and cold dips served with dipping chips and vegetables became very popular in the '50s because more people were eating in front of the TV and no utensils were required. I assure you that even now in the twenty-first century, this dip is still very popular here at my house and with my clients! Take it to any party and there's never any left in the dish!

INGREDIENTS

- 1 package frozen creamed spinach, thawed
- 1 can 14 oz. artichoke hearts, drained, chopped
- 1 cup good-quality mayonnaise
- 1 Tbs. Worcestershire
- 2 shakes of favorite hot sauce
- ½ tsp. garlic powder or granulated garlic
- 1–2 cups grated Parmesan or Pecorino Romano (or combo)
- Paprika for garnish

INSTRUCTIONS

1. Mix all ingredients thoroughly and put into a sprayed ovenproof container. Sprinkle with paprika (optional).
2. Bake in oven at 350 degrees for 25–30 minutes until hot and bubbly.

PERFECT PRIME RIB

PREP TIME: 5–10 Minutes
COOK/REST TIME: 3 ½ Hours
SERVES: Varies

Our dear friends, Ken and Shelley, invited us for a special prime rib dinner when I was in my twenties, and my mom went crazy for its luxurious taste and perfect medium-rare temperature. I have a copy of this recipe/guide with a handwritten note from Tutu that says, "DO NOT EVER THROW AWAY!" So I haven't, because it truly is the best. Thanks for sharing all those years ago, Ken.

INGREDIENTS

- 7–8 lb. bone-in prime rib roast (usually 3 rib bones)**
- Kosher salt or sea salt, coarsely ground
- Pepper, freshly cracked
- 4–6 fresh garlic cloves
- 3–4 stems fresh thyme or rosemary

HORSERADISH CREAM:

12 oz. sour cream or Greek yogurt
1–2 Tbs. horseradish
½ tsp. granulated garlic

INSTRUCTIONS

1. Season roast liberally with salt and pepper.
2. Peel and slice garlic. Using paring knife, make slits in top of roast and stuff with garlic slices.
3. Allow to sit at room temperature for about 1 hour.
4. Preheat oven to 375 degrees.
5. Place meat fat side up a shallow roasting pan and add fresh herbs
6. Meanwhile, mix sour cream, horseradish, and granulated garlic and place in refrigerator.
7. Bake uncovered for 1 hour.
8. Turn the oven off and let roast sit for 1.5 hours. Do not open the oven door. (We usually go to mass at this time on Christmas Eve.)
9. Turn oven back on to 375 degrees and roast for 30–40 minutes for medium rare to medium.
10. Serve with horseradish cream.

> **TIP**
> I like to have my butcher debone and tie the bone back on for roasting to get optimal flavor but easy carving.

CANDIED BACON

PREP TIME: 5 Minutes
COOK TIME: 20-30 Minutes
MAKES: 10-14 slices

This was not a recipe my mom made. However, it was my younger brother, Danny's, absolute favorite (he was a bacon *lover*), and he requested it for every special occasion. The combination of sweet, spicy, and salty is irresistible.

INGREDIENTS

- 1 lb. hickory or applewood smoked bacon
- 2 Tbs. hot sauce
- ⅓ cup brown sugar

INSTRUCTIONS

1. Preheat oven to 375 degrees.
2. Line a baking sheet with foil and lay bacon slices into single layer.
3. Mix brown sugar with hot sauce until smooth.
4. Brush brown sugar mixture over bacon and bake at 375-400 degrees for 20–30 minutes.
5. Watch closely the last 5 minutes, so as not to burn.
6. Allow to cool and crisp up a bit. Serve in a mason jar or a vase.

CAPTAIN LORD MANSION POTATOES

PREP TIME: 10 Minutes
COOK TIME: 55–58 Minutes
SERVES: 8–10

My dear sister-in-law Susie discovered this recipe at the Captain Lord Mansion bed and breakfast in Kennebunkport, Maine, while she and my brother David attended a wedding there. After she made this for us at their cabin, it became a family and friend brunch favorite and is demanded at my annual Girls' Annual Holiday Brunch.

INGREDIENTS

- 2 lb. bag frozen Southern-style hash brown potatoes
- ⅔ cup ranch dressing
- 10 ¾ oz. can cream of mushroom soup
- 10 ¾ oz. can cream of chicken soup
- 2 cups sharp cheddar cheese, grated
- ½ tsp. black pepper
- Couple dashes Worcestershire sauce
- 6 oz. can fried onion rings, crushed slightly

INSTRUCTIONS

1. Mix all ingredients together except for the onion rings.
2. Pour into a 9" x 13" baking dish that has been sprayed with cooking spray.
3. Bake at 350 degrees for 50 minutes.
4. Remove from oven and sprinkle with the crushed onion rings.
5. Return to oven and bake an additional 5–8 minutes or until onion rings are slightly browned and heated through.

CRAB RANGOONS

PREP TIME: 45 Minutes
COOK TIME: 2–3 Minutes
MAKES: About 4 Dozen

I learned how to make these at a cooking class in my late twenties. This recipe became a family holiday tradition beginning with our annual Ray/Lettieri Italian Christmas Party. Tutu would sit at the kitchen table and help me wrap literally dozens and dozens of these. My daughter, Taylor, has become an expert wrapper and has taken the reigns from her grandmother in helping to keep this delicious tradition alive. My dependable husband, Dave, has fried thousands of them over the years! Try them for your next holiday gathering or for a delicious treat for the New Year!

INGREDIENTS

- 8 oz. crabmeat or surimi (imitation crab)
- 8 oz. cream cheese (regular or low-fat)
- ½–1 tsp. salt
- ½ tsp. garlic powder or granulated garlic
- 1 tsp. fresh horseradish
- 1 12 oz. package won ton wrappers
- Vegetable oil
- Water

INSTRUCTIONS

1. In bowl or food processor, mix crabmeat, cream cheese, salt, garlic powder, and horseradish until well blended.
2. Set up "wrapping station" with small bowl of water, won ton wrappers, crab mixture, and two teaspoons. Use a cutting board and have a damp towel to cover won ton wrappers to keep them from drying out.
3. Lay a wrapper flat and wet the edges. Place a teaspoon of mixture into center and fold upward to form a triangle. Seal with fingers and then wet one of the horizontal points and pinch won ton together in center. Fry in small batches in 350-degree vegetable oil until golden brown.
4. Serve with Plum Dipping Sauce.

PLUM DIPPING SAUCE

This is a sweet and savory sauce perfect for dipping your crab rangoons into. It makes a large batch, so feel free to use as a dipping sauce for egg rolls or pot stickers, or as a glaze for ham, pork, or shrimp. It's also delicious over cream cheese with crackers. It will keep in the refrigerator for several weeks, or you can freeze some for later.

Prep Time: 10 minutes
1 can crushed pineapple, in syrup
1 cup sugar
1 cup water
1 cup white or rice vinegar
1 Tbs. soy sauce
2 Tbs. cornstarch
2 Tbs. cold water
1 cup plum jam

1. Heat pineapple (with syrup), sugar, water, vinegar, and soy sauce to boiling. Mix cornstarch and cold water into a slurry and stir gradually into mixture. Heat to a boil, stirring constantly.
2. Cool to room temperature; add plum jam and stir to combine. Cover and refrigerate.

SALTINE CRACKER TOFFEE

PREP TIME: 10 Minutes
COOK/SET TIME: 40 Minutes
MAKES: 2 Pounds

One year for Christmas, a friend of Taylor's gifted us with this special treat. Tutu took one piece and was immediately in love! It's been a holiday favorite ever since. Be careful; it's addictive!

INGREDIENTS

- 1 cup butter
- 1 cup dark or light brown sugar, packed
- 1 ½ sleeves (about 36) saltine crackers
- 1 cup semisweet chocolate chips
- 1 cup chopped pecans or nut of your choice

INSTRUCTIONS

1. Preheat oven to 350 degrees.
2. Line an 11" x 17" or 10" x 15" inch jelly roll pan with aluminum foil, tucking foil into edges and over sides. Spray generously with cooking spray.
3. Line jelly roll pan with saltines in one layer, placing crackers together tightly without overlapping. Break saltines in half to complete last row if needed.
4. In a small to medium saucepan, blend butter and brown sugar over medium-high to high heat until boiling, then turn down to a gentle rolling boil for about 4 minutes until bubbly and caramel colored. Pour evenly over saltines and carefully straighten any crackers that move.
5. Place in oven for 10 minutes. While waiting, chop nuts.
6. Remove from oven and immediately sprinkle with chocolate chips. Let stand 3–5 minutes until the chocolate melts and carefully spread with spatula evenly over toffee.
7. Sprinkle evenly with chopped nuts, carefully pressing them into chocolate
8. Place in refrigerator to chill for 30 minutes. Crack into pieces and place in airtight container.

MERINGUE DROPS (A.K.A. PAVLOVA)

PREP TIME: 10–15 Minutes
COOK TIME: 1 Hour
MAKES: 2–3 Dozen

These cookies were a holiday staple on the DeBard family cookie tray. Sometimes, we added chocolate chips and mint extract. These drop cookies are made of the same meringue used to make pavlova, which can be made into many fancy dessert displays. When I see them, I am reminded of the beautiful snowy Christmases of my childhood. Thanks to the talented Bouckaert cousins and baker and cook extraordinaire cousin Carrie (and family), for faithfully and lovingly keeping the holiday cookie traditions alive!

INGREDIENTS

- 4 room-temperature egg whites
- ¼ tsp. cream of tartar or meringue powder
- ⅛ tsp. salt (a dash)
- 1 tsp. vanilla extract or mint extract
- 1 cup sugar
- ½ cup semisweet chocolate chips (optional)

INSTRUCTIONS

1. Preheat oven to 225 degrees.
2. Line two cookie sheets with foil or parchment paper.
3. In a mixing bowl, beat egg whites, cream of tartar, and salt at high speed until soft peaks form. Gradually add extract and sugar, 2 tablespoons at a time.
4. Continue beating for about 5 minutes until sugar is completely dissolved and stiff peaks form.
5. Fold in chocolate chips (if using).
6. Drop by teaspoonfuls onto cookie sheets and bake for 1 hour, being careful not to open the oven door in the meantime. (Option: use a piping bag and pipe out for a fancier look.)
7. These should be stored in a tin in a cool, dry place.

TUTU'S PANTRY STAPLES
CIRCA 1970s

Tutu cooked for our family during an era of convenience grocery items and embraced them to help her get meals on the table quicker and more efficiently. I wouldn't call them "healthy" choices by today's standards, but they were fitting back then, considering the limited time and budget of a single mom. We always had seasonal garden and farm-fresh produce available to us like asparagus, blueberries, corn, strawberries, squash, greens, rhubarb, tomatoes, radishes, cucumbers, apples, cherries, celery, carrots, and peppers, which provided nutrition and variety.

1. REAL BUTTER
   (and a stick of butter on the counter, always softened and ready to spread)
2. MAYONNAISE
   (I'm a Duke's girl now.)
3. LAWRY'S SEASONED SALT
4. CELERY AND CARROTS
   (cleaned, peeled, cut up, and salted in a plastic container)
5. GREEN PEPPER AND ONION
6. CHEESE
   (cheddar, Kraft Grated Parmesan Cheese, and American slices, but she wasn't too good for a block of Velveeta or a jar of Cheez Whiz)
7. CANNED MEAT
   (Spam, tuna, Braunschweiger. etc.)
8. SALTINES/CRACKERS
9. WONDER BREAD
10. CREAM-BASED SOUPS
11. BOXED CAKE MIXES
12. BISQUICK
13. CRISCO
14. CANNED (PREFERABLY STEWED) TOMATOES
15. PASTA/MACARONI
16. JELL-O
17. KRAFT MACARONI AND CHEESE
18. BLUEBERRY MUFFIN MIX
19. HAMBURGER HELPER
20. CEREAL
21. SQUEEZE CHEESE
22. CANNED MUSHROOMS
23. PEANUT BUTTER AND JELLY
24. LOVE

Tutu didn't have a lot of kitchen appliances or gadgets, but a few basics sufficed and she was able to make fabulous meals. One of her closest friends, "Aunt Donna," gave her a hand-me-down microwave in the late '70s, and my mom was fascinated with it! It was by far her favorite modern kitchen convenience in appliances. But, oh, was it BIG!

ABOUT THE AUTHOR

Jill Aker-Ray is a personal chef who specializes in vacations and family milestones. She treats every meal or gathering as a special celebration, a trait she learned from her mother.

Jill has appeared on television stations nationwide, sharing her cooking skills along with simple entertaining tips and hacks. She is a regular contributor on popular Charlotte-area television stations, WCNC and WBTV.

In her spare time, Jill enjoys travel and discovering and exploring new places, cultures, food, and wine. Her happy place is on the beach or poolside with a good book and a cold beverage. She says the best part of being a traveling chef is the opportunity to explore new flavors at vacation hotspots across the United States, Canada and the Caribbean.

Aker-Ray never turns down a chance to gather with friends and family over a game or puzzle. In her downtime, she loves to snuggle with her Great Dane, Luna, sharing a bowl of buttered popcorn while bingeing on Netflix!

This is Jill's first cookbook, and it is dedicated to her mom, a.k.a. "Tutu," who was the master of making every occasion a party!

ABOUT THE PHOTOGRAPHER

A devoted food enthusiast, Stacey Sprenz believes that food photography is more than photos of beautifully plated meals.

It begins with a deep passion for our food communities; a love for the people who create and cultivate those communities; and the drive to tell the story of people, food, and community. As a freelance photographer based in Durham, NC, Stacey delights in using photography to tell food stories and help artisans market their products and services. Her work allows her to be immersed in the food and beverage scene in various ways including through photography/ food styling, recipe development, and teaching food photography workshops.

INDEX

Index

CPSIA information can be obtained
at www.ICGtesting.com
Printed in the USA
LVRC090115120422
715935LV00004B/8